T0113985

THE HISTORY MANIFESTO

How should historians speak truth to power – and why does it matter? Why is five hundred years better than five months or five years as a planning horizon? And why is history – especially long-term history – so essential to understanding the multiple pasts which gave rise to our conflicted present? *The History Manifesto* is a call to arms to historians and everyone interested in the role of history in contemporary society. Leading historians Jo Guldi and David Armitage identify a recent shift back to longer-term narratives, following many decades of increasing specialisation, which they argue is vital for the future of historical scholarship and how it is communicated. This provocative and thoughtful book makes an important intervention in the debate about the role of history and the humanities in a digital age. It will provoke discussion among policy-makers, activists, and entrepreneurs as well as ordinary listeners, viewers, readers, students, and teachers.

JO GULDI is the Hans Rothfels Assistant Professor of History at Brown University. She is the author of *Roads to Power: Britain Invents the Infrastructure State* (2012).

DAVID ARMITAGE is the Lloyd C. Blankfein Professor of History at Harvard University. Among his publications are *The Ideological Origins of the British Empire* (2000), *Foundations of Modern International Thought* (2013), *Milton and Republicanism* (co-edited, 1995), *Bolingbroke: Political Writings* (edited, 1997), *British Political Thought in History, Literature and Theory, 1500-1800* (co-edited, 2006), and *Shakespeare and Early Modern Political Thought* (co-edited, 2009), all from Cambridge University Press.

'This is a very important and refreshing book. For too long, we have seen increasing specialisation within historical research and between the disciplines of social sciences. Armitage and Guldi rightly plead for a return of the *longue durée*. They call for more global, long-run and transdisciplinary approaches to big questions, including climate change, inequality and the future of capitalism. Their book will be an important milestone in this direction. A must read.'

Thomas Piketty,
Paris School of Economics

'This well-written, smart, deeply and broadly learned book is a bracing challenge to contemporary historiography. Critical of the loss of a sense of *la longue durée* and series, replaced by histories of the "short term" and micro-scale since the 1970s, the authors argue that history has lost much of its public significance and usefulness. David Armitage and Jo Guldi have produced a rich history of the discipline as the foundation of a compelling plea for bringing forth more, bigger and better histories into our civic life.'

Thomas Bender,
New York University

'Guldi and Armitage make a compelling argument for the relevance of history, and for its potential as an antidote to the twin afflictions of short-term thinking and future prognostication based on poor or partial evidence. In a concise and clear book, they make renewed claims for the capacity of the past and its data, properly studied, to inform public policy and democratic debate on a wide range of issues from economic malfunction to climate change. They also throw out a challenge to academic historians to pull on, and perhaps break, some disciplinary shackles that have mentally fettered the profession for the better part of a century.'

Daniel Woolf,
Queen's University, Ontario

'How can we think seriously about our grandchildren's future if no one thinks on scales longer than a few years? Jo Guldi and David Armitage tell a rich and swashbuckling story of how historians are returning to big-picture thinking, armed now with the rich insights of microhistory and the vast archives of big data. In the Age of the Anthropocene, they argue, it is vital that we know the past, and that we know it at very large scales.'

David Christian,
Macquarie University

'History will always remain a craft with many workshops perfecting different traditions, but here is a fast-paced manifesto which urges the profession to focus on long-term questions and embrace ethical obligations to provide urgently needed perspectives on key dilemmas of our times. Its view of recent Anglo-American historiography as "short-termist" and passionate plea that history can map out alternative possibilities for better societies will invite controversy and instantly invigorate classroom debates with a double shot.'

Ulinka Rublack,
University of Cambridge, and editor of A Concise Companion to History

'An important attempt to make history relevant to a broad public, away from the narrow specialisation that has dominated the historical profession to a long-range nexus of past, present and future which places the present global crises of ecology and inequality in their historical context and takes into account the impact of digitalisation on historical studies.'

Georg G. Iggers,
University at Buffalo, The State University of New York

'An exhilarating anticipation of a digitised and globalised future, in which historians will assume the role of critical problem-solver. Guldi and Armitage argue that to do so, historians must recover their command of the *longue durée* and boldly apply their grasp of multi-causality to the dominant practical disciplines of the day.'

John Tosh,
University of Roehampton

'In their timely and useful book, Armitage and Guldi have issued a call to arms. They urge historians to use their knowledge and skills to think big, to embrace long-term thinking and the possibilities of digital technology. Above all they hope that an increasingly fragmented discipline can embrace its public role and take on, in an ethical, utopian spirit, some of the biggest issues of our time, such as inequality and climate change. They make a heartfelt plea for those who specialise in the past to make a major contribution to thinking about the future. Their manifesto for history as a critical social science deserves careful consideration both by those already persuaded of its public purpose and by those yet to embrace this generous view of the field.'

Ludmilla Jordanova,
Durham University

'Of all the many ways in which public policies and public debates today lack necessary perspective, perhaps the most important is their lack of historical perspective. In *The History Manifesto* David Armitage and Jo Guldi offer a ringing call not just for more knowledge of the past, but for the centrality of a broad and deep understanding of history to public knowledge itself.'

Craig Calhoun,
London School of Economics and Political Science

'Big problems meet big data in this compelling case for long-term thinking in the public sphere. Guldi and Armitage don't just chart a new course for the discipline of history, but for the *uses* of history across disciplines. I'm convinced: a return to the *longue durée* is theoretically sound, technologically feasible, politically imperative.'

Bethany Nowviskie,
University of Virginia

'Ideas about big and deep histories have been recently flagged as ways historians could make their work speak to present concerns about human futures. This wide-ranging and spirited book not only provides the best discussion so far of these questions; by staking the very future of history on historians' capacity to shape public debates, Guldi and Armitage issue to fellow historians nothing short of a stirring call to action. A welcome and timely intervention.'

Dipesh Chakrabarty,
University of Chicago

THE HISTORY MANIFESTO

JO GULDI

Brown University

and

DAVID ARMITAGE

Harvard University

CAMBRIDGE
UNIVERSITY PRESS

University Printing House, Cambridge CB2 8BS, United Kingdom

One Liberty Plaza, 20th Floor, New York, NY 10006, USA

477 Williamstown Road, Port Melbourne, VIC 3207, Australia

314-321, 3rd Floor, Plot 3, Splendor Forum, Jasola District Centre, New Delhi - 110025, India

103 Penang Road, #05-06/07, Visioncrest Commercial, Singapore 238467

Cambridge University Press is part of the University of Cambridge.

It furthers the University's mission by disseminating knowledge in the pursuit of education, learning and research at the highest international levels of excellence.

www.cambridge.org
Information on this title: www.cambridge.org/9781107432437

First published 2014
6th printing 2019

Reprinted with corrections; for a full list of corrections please see
https://www.cambridge.org/core/what-we-publish/open-access/the-history-manifesto

A catalogue record for this publication is available from the British Library

Library of Congress Cataloging in Publication data
Guldi, Jo (Joanna), 1978–
The history manifesto / Jo Guldi (Brown University) and David Armitage (Harvard University).
pages cm
Includes bibliographical references and index.
ISBN 978-1-107-07634-1 (Hardback) – ISBN 978-1-107-43243-7 (Paperback)
1. History–Philosophy. 2. Historiography–Philosophy. 3. Historiography–Political aspects. 4. Historiography–Social aspects. I. Armitage, David, 1965– II. Title.
D16.8.G85 2014
901–dc23 2014027869

ISBN 978-1-107-07634-1 Hardback
ISBN 978-1-107-43243-7 Paperback

Additional resources for this publication at historymanifesto.cambridge.org

Contents

List of figures   *page* viii
Acknowledgements   ix

Introduction: the bonfire of the humanities?   I

1   Going forward by looking back: the rise of the *longue durée*   14

2   The short past: or, the retreat of the *longue durée*   38

3   The long and the short: climate change, governance,
    and inequality since the 1970s   61

4   Big questions, big data   88

Conclusion: the public future of the past   117

Notes   126
Index   161

Figures

1 Usage of 'short-termism', *c.* 1975–2000   *page* 2
2 Number of years covered in History dissertations in
   the United States, *c.* 1885–2012   44
3 Usage of 'more and more about less [and less]', 1900–90   49
4 Relative prominence of mentions of India, Ireland, and
   other topics in relationship to each other, 1880–1980   92

Acknowledgements

The History Manifesto arose from many discussions about the future of history, the return of the *longue durée*, and the role of academics in public culture. Jo Guldi recalls Jeremy DuQuesnay Adams and David Nirenberg planting the seeds for the argument of the book; David Armitage likewise remembers exchanges with Alison Bashford and Darrin McMahon as pivotal for his own thinking. Conversation led to collaboration; a seminar-paper turned into an article; the article expanded into this book. We sandwiched work on it between many other personal and professional commitments: for their patience and support, Jo Guldi thanks especially Zachary Gates while David Armitage salutes the staff of the History Department at Harvard University. We are both grateful to Zachary Davis for efficient and imaginative research assistance.

We presented earlier versions of parts of our argument at Yale Law School, to the History Department at Brown University, and at Reid Hall in Paris. We are very grateful to the audiences on those occasions for their comments and encouragement, as well as to Jenny Andersson, Margy Avery, Omer Bartov, Peter Burke, Jennifer Burns, Harold Cook, Simon DeDeo, Matt Desmond, Paul Freedman, Stella Ghervas, John Gillis, Tom Griffiths, Lynn Hunt, Daniel Jütte, Jeremy Kessler, Dan Smail, Anna Su, John Witt, and Daniel Woolf for their reactions and responses. Our thanks also go to the editors of *Annales*, especially Etienne Anheim and Antoine Lilti, for help with an essay in their journal which draws upon material from Chapters 1 and 2.

The History Manifesto has been an unusually collaborative book, not just for the authors, but between them and Cambridge University Press. Richard Fisher, publishing visionary *extraordinaire*, supported our mission from the very beginning and from the summit of the Press. Without Liz Friend-Smith's editorial energy, enthusiasm, and élan, the book would not have been started and certainly would not have been finished. Christina Sarigiannidou and Rosalyn Scott shepherded an unprecedentedly intense production schedule with calm and grace, Barbara Docherty was a model copy-editor during the same mad dash to the finish-line, and Caroline Diepeveen produced an excellent index in record time. The Press's commitment throughout to open-access and online publication of *The History Manifesto* has been both innovative and inspirational. We welcome the broader discussion this experiment will open up: please join the conversation at historymanifesto.cambridge.org.

JO GULDI,
Providence, RI
DAVID ARMITAGE,
Sydney
July 2014

Introduction
The bonfire of the humanities?

A spectre is haunting our time: the spectre of the short term.

We live in a moment of accelerating crisis that is characterised by the shortage of long-term thinking. Even as rising sea-levels threaten low-lying communities and coastal regions, the world's cities stockpile waste, and human actions poison the oceans, earth, and groundwater for future generations. We face rising economic inequality within nations even as inequalities between countries abate while international hierarchies revert to conditions not seen since the late eighteenth century, when China last dominated the global economy. Where, we might ask, is safety, where is freedom? What place will our children call home? There is no public office of the long term that you can call for answers about who, if anyone, is preparing to respond to these epochal changes. Instead, almost every aspect of human life is plotted and judged, packaged and paid for, on timescales of a few months or years. There are few opportunities to shake those projects loose from their short-term moorings. It can hardly seem worth while to raise questions of the long term at all.

In the age of the permanent campaign, politicians plan only as far as their next bid for election. They invoke children and grandchildren in public speeches, but electoral cycles of two to seven years determine which issues prevail. The result is less money for crumbling infrastructure and schools and more for any initiative that promises jobs right now. The same short horizons govern the way most corporate boards organise their futures. Quarterly cycles mean that executives have to show profit on a regular basis.[1] Long-term investments in human resources disappear from the balance sheet, and so they are cut. International institutions, humanitarian bodies, and non-governmental organisations (NGOs) must follow the same logic and adapt their programmes to annual or at most triennial constraints. No one, it seems, from bureaucrats to board members, or voters and recipients of international aid, can escape the ever-present threat of short-termism.

There are individuals who buck the trend, of course. In 1998, the Californian cyber-utopian Stewart Brand created the Long Now Foundation to promote consciousness of broader spans of time. 'Civilization is revving itself into a pathologically short attention span', he wrote: 'Some sort of balancing corrective to the short-sightedness is needed – some mechanism or myth that encourages the long view and the taking of long-term responsibility, where "the long term" is measured at least in centuries.' Brand's charismatic solution to the problem of short-termism is the Clock of the Long Now, a mechanism operating on a computational span of 10,000 years designed precisely to measure time in centuries, even millennia.[2]

But the lack of long-range perspective in our culture remains. The disease even has a name – 'short-termism'. Short-termism has many practitioners but few defenders. It is now so deeply ingrained in our institutions that it has become a habit – frequently followed but rarely justified, much complained about but not often diagnosed. It was only given a name, at least in English, in the 1980s, after which usage sky-rocketed significantly (see Figure 1).

The most ambitious diagnosis of short-termism to date came from the Oxford Martin Commission for Future Generations. In October 2013, a blue-ribbon panel chaired by Pascal Lamy, former Director-General of the World Trade Organization (WTO), issued its report, *Now for the Long Term*, 'focusing on the increasing short-termism of modern politics and our collective inability to break the gridlock

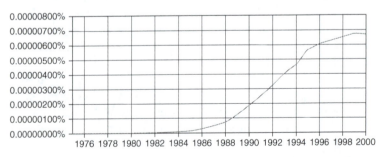

Figure 1 Usage of 'short-termism', *c.* 1975–2000
Source: Google Ngram viewer.

which undermines attempts to address the biggest challenges that will shape our future'. Though the tone of the report was hardly upbeat, its thrust was forward-looking and future-oriented. Its motto might have been the words quoted in its introduction and attributed to former French premier Pierre Mendès France: *gouverner, c'est prévoir* – to govern is to foresee.[3]

Imagining the long term as an alternative to the short term may not be so difficult, but putting long-termism into practice may be harder to achieve. When institutions or individuals want to peer into the future, there is a dearth of knowledge about how to go about this task. Instead of facts, we routinely resort to theories. We have been told, for instance, that there was an end to history and that the world is hot, flat, and crowded.[4] We have read that all human events are reducible to models derived from physics, translated by economics or political science, or explained by a theory of evolution that looks back to our hunter-gatherer ancestors. Editorials apply economic models to sumo wrestlers and palaeolithic anthropology to customs of dating.[5] These lessons are repeated on the news, and their proponents are elevated to the status of public intellectuals. Their rules seem to point to unchanging levers that govern our world. But they do little to explain the shifting hierarchy of economies or the changes in gender identity and reconfigurations of banking witnessed in our own time. Only in rare conversations does anyone notice that there are long-term changes flowing around us, ones that are relevant and possible to see. The world around us is clearly one of change, irreducible to models. Who is trained to steadily wait upon and translate them for others, these vibrations of deeper time?

Even those who have assigned themselves the task of inspecting the future typically peer only shortsightedly into the past. Stewart Brand's Clock of the Long Now points 10,000 years ahead but looks barely a century backwards. The Martin Commission searched for evidence for various 'megatrends' – among them, population growth, shifts in migration, employment, inequality, sustainability, and health care – but the Commission included no historians to tell them how much these trends had changed over a lifespan, or the truly long-term of centuries or millennia. In fact, few of the examples the Commission cited in *Now for the Long Term* came from before the late 1940s. Most of the evidence entertained by these self-proclaimed futurologists came from the last thirty years, even though the relevant section of the report carried the title, 'Looking Back to Look Forward'. Such historical myopia is itself a symptom of the short-termism they are trying to overcome.

Indeed, the world around us is hungry for long-term thinking. In political science departments and over dinner tables, citizens around the world complain about political stagnation and the limits of two-party systems. A lack of serious alternatives to *laissez-faire* capitalism is the hallmark of contemporary world governance from the World Bank to the WTO. Currencies, nations, and sea-levels fall and rise. Even the professions in advanced economies that garnered the most secure jobs a generation ago are no longer stable. What sort of an education prepares individuals for so volatile a run through the journey of life? How does a young person come to learn not only to listen and to communicate, but also to judge institutions, to see which technologies hold promise and which are doomed to fail, to think fluidly about state and market and the connections between both? And how can they do so with an eye to where we have come from, as well as where we are going to?

*****

Thinking about the past in order to see the future is not actually so difficult. Most of us become aware of change first in the family, as we regard the omnipresent tensions between one generation and the next. In even these familial exchanges, we look backwards in order to see the future. Nimble people, whether activists or entrepreneurs, likewise depend on an instinctual sense of change from past to present to future as they navigate through their day-to-day activities. Noticing a major shift in the economy before one's contemporaries may result in the building of fortunes, as is the case for the real estate speculator who notices rich people moving to a former ghetto before other developers. Noticing a shift in politics, an amassing of unprecedented power by corporations and the repeal of earlier legislation, is what precipitated a movement like Occupy Wall Street. Regardless of age or security of income, we are all in the business of making sense of a changing world. In all cases, understanding the nexus of past and future is crucial to acting upon what comes next.

But who writes about these changes as long-term developments? Who nourishes those looking for brighter futures with the material from our collective past? Centuries and epochs are often mysteries too deep and wide for journalists to concern themselves with. Only in rare conversations does anyone notice that there are continuities that are relevant and possible to see. Who is trained to wait steadily upon these vibrations of deeper time and then translate them for others?

Universities have a special claim as venues for thinking on longer time scales. Historically, universities have been among the most resilient, enduring, and long-lasting institutions humans have created. Nalanda University in Bihar, India, was founded over 1500 years ago as a Buddhist institution and is now being revived again as a seat of learning. The great European foundations of Bologna (1088), Paris (c. 1150), Oxford (1167), Cambridge (1209), Salamanca (1218), Toulouse (1229), and Heidelberg (1386), to name only a few, date back to the eleventh to the fourteenth centuries, and there were universities in mid sixteenth-century Peru and Mexico decades before Harvard or Yale was chartered. By contrast, the average half-life of a twentieth-century business corporation has been calculated at seventy-five years: there may be only two companies in the world that can compare with most universities for longevity.[6]

Universities, along with religious institutions, are the carriers of traditions, the guardians of deep knowledge. They should be the centres of innovation where research takes place without regard to profit or immediate application.[7] Precisely that relative disinterestedness has given the university particular room to ponder long-term questions using long-term resources. As the vice-chancellor of the oldest university in Oceania, the University of Sydney (1850), has noted, universities remain 'the one player capable of making long-term, infrastructure-intensive research investments ... Business generally seeks return on investment over a period of a few years. If universities take a similar approach, there will simply be no other entities globally capable of supporting research on 20-, 30-, or 50-year time horizons.'[8]

Yet the peculiar capacity of the university to foster disinterested inquiries into the long term may be as endangered as long-term thinking itself. For most of the history of universities, the responsibility for passing on tradition and subjecting it to critical examination has been borne by the humanities.[9] These subjects now include the study of languages, literature, art, music, philosophy, and history, but in their original conception extended to all non-professional subjects, including logic and rhetoric, but excluding law, medicine, and theology. Their educational purpose was precisely not to be instrumental: to examine theories and instances, to pose questions and the means of their solution, but not to propose practical objectives or strategies. As the medieval university mutated into the modern research university, and as private foundations become subject to public control and funding, the goals of the humanities were increasingly tested and contested. For at least the last century, wherever the humanities have been taught or studied there has been debate about their 'relevance' and their 'value'. Crucial to the defence of the humanities has been their mission to transmit questions about value – and to question values – over hundreds, even thousands, of years. Any search for antidotes to short-termism must begin with them.

Yet everywhere we turn the humanities are said to be in 'crisis': more specifically, the former president of the American Historical Association, Lynn Hunt, has recently argued that the field of 'history is in crisis and not just one of university budgets'.[10] There is nothing new in this: the advantage of a historical perspective is knowing that the humanities have been in recurrent crisis for the last fifty years at least. The threats have varied from country to country and from decade to decade but some of the enemies are consistent. The humanities can appear 'soft' and indistinct in their findings compared to the so-called 'hard' sciences. They can seem to be a luxury, even an indulgence, in contrast to disciplines oriented towards professional careers, like economics or law. They rarely compete in the push to recruit high-profit relationships with software, engineering, and pharmaceutical clientele. And they can be vulnerable to new technologies that might render the humanities' distinctive methods, such as close reading of texts, an appreciation for abstract values, and the promotion of critical thinking over instrumental reasoning jejune. The humanities are incidental (not instrumental), obsolescent (not effervescent), increasingly vulnerable (not technologically adaptable) – or so their enemies and sceptics would have us believe.[11]

The crisis of the university has become acute for several reasons. The accumulation and dissemination of knowledge through teaching and publishing is undergoing changes more profound than at any point in the last five hundred years. In many parts of the world, but especially in North America, parents and students have inherited a university retooled into a specialised engine of expertise, often dominated by the star disciplines of physics, economics, and neuroscience, designed to manufacture articles at record numbers, and often insensitive to other traditions of learning. The latest 'crisis of the humanities' has been much discussed and its causes broadly debated. Enrolments in humanities courses have apparently declined from historic highs. Massive open online courses (MOOCs) seemed to portend the extinction of small-group teaching and the intimate process of interaction between teachers and students. The shifting boundaries between humanistic and scientific disciplines can make this manner of engaging the humanities seem quaint or superfluous. Squeezes on public revenues and private endowments create pressures from outside universities to deliver value and from inside them to demonstrate viability. For teachers of the humanities, battling these challenges from within and from without can feel like a struggle against the many-headed Hydra: Herculean – and therefore heroic – but unremitting, because every victory brings with it a new adversary.

Administrators, academics, and students alike struggle to face all these challenges at once. They must strive to find a way forward that will preserve the distinctive virtues of the university – and of the humanities and historical social sciences within them. Importantly, they need experts who can look past the parochial concerns of disciplines too attached to client funding, the next business cycle, or the next election. Indeed, in a crisis of short-termism, our world needs somewhere to turn to for information about the relationship between past and future. Our argument is that History – the discipline and its subject-matter – can be just the arbiter we need at this critical time.

*****

Any broader public looking for solutions to short-termism in the History departments of most universities might have been quite disappointed, at least until very recently. As we document in later chapters, historians once told arching stories of scale but, nearly forty years ago, many if not most of them stopped doing so. For two generations, between about 1975 and 2005, they conducted most of their studies on biological time-spans of between five and fifty years, approximating the length of a mature human life. The compression of time in historical work can be illustrated bluntly by the range covered in doctoral dissertations conducted in the United States, a country which adopted the German model of doctoral education early and then produced history doctorates on a world-beating scale. In 1900, the average number of years covered in doctoral dissertations in history in the United States was about seventy-five years; by 1975, it was closer to thirty. Command of archives; total control of a ballooning historiography; and an imperative to reconstruct and analyse in ever-finer detail: all these had become the hallmarks of historical professionalism. Later in the book, we will document why and how this concentration – some might say, contraction – of time took place. For the moment, it is enough to note that short-termism had become an academic pursuit as well as a public problem in the last quarter of the twentieth century.

It was during this period, we argue, that professional historians ceded the task of synthesising historical knowledge to unaccredited writers and simultaneously lost whatever influence they might once have had over policy to colleagues in the social sciences, most spectacularly to the economists. The gulf between academic and non-academic history widened. After 2000 years, the ancient goal for history to be the guide to public life had collapsed. With the 'telescoping of historical time … the discipline of history, in a peculiar way, ceased to be historical'.[12] History departments lay increasingly exposed to new and unsettling challenges: the recurrent crises of the humanities marked by waning enrolments; ever more invasive demands from administrators and their political paymasters to demonstrate 'impact'; and internal crises of confidence about their relevance amid adjacent disciplines with swelling classrooms, greater visibility, and more obvious influence in shaping public opinion.

But there are now signs that the long term and the long range are returning. The scope of doctoral dissertations in history is already widening. Professional historians are again writing monographs covering periods of 200 to 2000 years or more. And there is now an expanding universe of historical horizons, from the 'deep history' of the human past, stretching over 40,000 years, to 'big history' going back to the Big Bang, 13.8 billion years ago. Across many fields of history, big is definitely back.[13] The return of the *longue durée* is how we describe the extension of historians' time-scales we both diagnose and recommend in this book.[14] In the last decade, across the university, the rise of big data and problems such as long-term climate change, governance, and inequality are causing a return to questions about how the past develops over centuries and millennia, and what this can tell us about our survival and flourishing in the future. This has brought a new sense of responsibility, as well as urgency, to the work of historians who 'should recognize that how they tell the story of the past shapes how the present understands its potential, and is thus an intervention in the future of the world', as one practitioner of history's public future has noted.[15]

The form and epistemology of these studies is not new. The *longue durée* as a term of historical art was the invention of the great French historian Fernand Braudel just over fifty years ago, in 1958.[16] As a temporal horizon for research and writing the *longue durée* largely disappeared for a generation before coming back into view in recent years. As we hope to suggest, the reasons for its retreat were sociological as much as intellectual; the motivations for its return are both political and technological. Yet the revenant *longue durée* is not identical to its original incarnation: as the French sociologist Pierre Bourdieu classically noted, 'returns to past styles are never "the same thing" since they are separated from what they return to by a negative reference to something which was itself the negation of it (or the negation of the negation)'.[17] The new *longue durée* has emerged within a very different ecosystem of intellectual alternatives. It possesses a dynamism and flexibility earlier versions did not have. It has a new relationship to the abounding sources of big data available in our time – data ecological, governmental, economic, and cultural in nature, much of it newly available to the lens of digital analysis. As a result of this increased reserve of evidence, the new *longue durée* also has greater critical potential, for historians, for other social scientists, for policy-makers, and for the public.

The origins of this new *longue durée* may lie in the past but it is now very much oriented towards the future. In this sense, it does mark a return to some of the foundations of historical thinking, in the West and in other parts of the world. Until history became professionalised as an academic discipline, with departments, journals, accrediting associations, and all the other formal trappings of a profession, its mission had been primarily educative, even reformative. History explained communities to themselves. It helped rulers to orient their exercise of power and in turn advised their advisors how to influence their superiors. And it provided citizens more generally with the coordinates by which they could understand the present and direct their actions towards the future. The mission for history as a guide to life never entirely lapsed. Increasing professionalism, and the explosion of scholarly publishing by historians within universities, obscured and at times occluded its purpose. But now it is returning along with the *longue durée* and the expansion of possibilities – for new research and novel public engagement – that accompanies it.

*****

We have organised this short book about the long term into two halves, each of two chapters. The first half maps the rise and fall of long-term thinking among historians; the second, its return and potential future as a critical human science. Chapter 1 traces the fortunes of two trends in historical writing and thinking over a *longue durée* of centuries and then a shorter span of decades. The initial trend is history's purpose as a guide to action in the present, using the resources of the past, to imagine alternative possibilities in the future. The other tendency is the more recent genesis of an explicit history of the *longue durée*, particularly in the work of the highly influential group of French historians associated in the twentieth century with the journal *Annales*. Pre-eminent among them was Fernand Braudel, the greatest proponent of his own peculiar but enduring conception of what the *longue durée* meant, in terms of time, movement, human agency (or the lack of it), and human interaction with the physical environment and the structural cycles of economics and politics. Building on earlier models of the *longue durée,* in this chapter, we set forward three approaches that history offers to those in need of a future: a sense of destiny and free will, counterfactual thinking, and thinking about utopias. Those freedoms of history, as we shall show in the chapters ahead, set aside historical thinking from the natural-law models of evolutionary anthropologists, economists, and other arbiters of our society. They are a crucial remedy for a society paralysed by short-term thinking, because these future-oriented tools of history open up new patterns of imagination with which to understand possible futures.

Almost as soon as the *longue durée* was named, it began to dissipate, as we show in Chapter 2. From the 1970s to the early twenty-first century, historians across the world began to focus on shorter time-scales. Their motivations were various. Some turned to the command of archives in order the better to fulfil the requirements of professionalisation; others to experiment with theories imported from neighbouring disciplines; still others, because professionalisation and theory offered a safe zone for writing out of their political commitments to radical causes that coincided with contemporary movements: in the United States especially, the Civil Rights movement, anti-war protest, or feminism. Out of these various desires, a new kind of history was born, one that concentrated on the 'micro-history' of exceptional individuals, seemingly inexplicable events, or significant conjunctures.

Micro-history was not invented to kill historical relevance but, as we shall see, even historians are haunted by the law of unintended consequences. Dedicated to the cause of testing and debunking larger theories about the nature of time and agency, historians in the English-speaking world who adopted the techniques of micro-history often concentrated upon writing for readers or communities only just finding their political voices. In the process, these micro-historians found themselves bound up with another larger contemporary force in intellectual life: the inward turn of academics towards an ever greater specialisation of knowledge. Still passionate about reform within their activist cells, micro-historians were increasingly rare in conversations about the old ambition of the university to be a guide to public life and possible futures. They were not the only ones. What have been called 'grand narratives' – big structures, large processes, and huge comparisons – were becoming increasingly unfashionable, and not just among historians. Big-picture thinking was widely perceived to be in retreat. Meanwhile, short-termism was on the rise.

One consequence of the retreat of historians from the public sphere was that institutions were taken over by other scholars, whose views of the past were determined less by historical data and more by universal models. Notably, this meant the rising profile of economists. As we show in Chapter 3, economists were everywhere – advising policies on the Left, advising policies on the Right; arbitrating grand debates in world government; even talking about the heritage of our hunter-gatherer ancestors and how their economic rationality determined our present and our future. In at least three spheres – discussions of climate, discussions of world government, and discussions of inequality – economists' universalising models came to dominate conversations about the future. At the end of Chapter 3, we set out the reasons that these views of human nature as static, not historical, are limiting. We outline an alternative approach to the future, and we recommend three modes of thinking about a future that we think good history does well: it looks at processes that take a long time to unfold; it engages false myths about the future and talks about where the data come from; and it looks to many different kinds and sources of data for multiple perspectives on how past and future were and may yet be experienced by a variety of different actors.

We partially explain what is replacing climate apocalypticism and economic predestination in Chapter 4, where we argue that short-term thinking is being challenged by the information technology of our time: the explosion of big data and the means now available to make sense of it all. Here we highlight the ways that scholars, businesses, activists, and historians are using new datasets to aggregate information about the history of inequality and the climate and to project new possible futures. We foreground the particular tools, many of them designed by historians, which are enhancing these datasets and drawing out qualitative models of changing thought over time. We show that this new data for thinking about the past and the future is rapidly outpacing the old analytics of economics, whose indicators were developed between the 1930s and the 1950s to measure the consumption and employment habits of people who lived very differently than we will in the twenty-first century. In coming decades, information scientists, environmentalists, and even financial analysts will increasingly need to think about when their data came from if they want to peer into the future. This change in the life of data may determine a major shift for the university of the future, where historical thinkers will have an increasingly important role to play as the arbiters of big data.

Our Conclusion ends where we started, with the problem of who in our society is responsible for constructing and interpreting the big picture. We are writing at a moment of the destabilisation of nations and currencies, on the cusp of a chain of environmental events that will change our way of life, at a time when questions of inequality trouble political and economic systems around the globe. On the basis of when we write, we recommend to our readers and to our fellow-historians the cause of what we call *the public future*: we must, all of us, engage the big picture, and do so together, a task that we believe requires us to look backwards as well as ahead.

The sword of history has two edges, one that cuts open new possibilities in the future, and one that cuts through the noise, contradictions, and lies of the past. In the Conclusion, we will claim that history offers three further indispensable means for looking at the past, which have more to do with history's power to sort truth from falsehood when we speak about our past and present situation. This sorting out of truth is part of the legacy of micro-historical examination, but it pertains equally to problems of big data; in both cases, historians have become adept at examining the basis of claims. History's power to liberate, we argue, ultimately lies in explaining where things came from, tacking between big processes and small events to see the whole picture, and reducing a lot of information to a small and shareable version. We recommend these methods to a society plagued by false ideas about the past and how it limits our collective hopes for the future.

There is never a problem with short-term thinking until short-termism predominates in a crisis. By implication, never before now has it been so vital that we all become experts on the long-term view, that we return to the *longue durée*. Renewing the connection between past and future, and using the past to think critically about what is to come, are the tools that we need now. Historians are those best able to supply them.

CHAPTER I

Going forward by looking back: the rise of the longue durée

The discipline of history holds particular promise for looking both backwards and forwards. After all, historians are masters of change over time. Over at least the last five hundred years, historians have among other things spoken truth to power, they have been reformers and leaders of the state, and they have revealed the worst abuses of corrupt institutions to public examination.[1] 'The longer you can look back the further you can look forward', said a mid twentieth-century master of political power who was also a prolific historian, Winston Churchill.[2]

Historians' expertise in long-term change gives them powers of contextualising events and processes that strike others as perhaps too ancient to be subject to question, too vast for curiosity to query. For historians, however, the shape of manners and the habits of institutions appear otherwise. Preferences and habits alike change from generation to generation; they are reformed entirely over the course of centuries.[3] Historians focus on the question of how: Who did the changing, and how can we be sure they were the agents? These analytics of causality, action, and consequence make them specialists in noticing the change around us.

Historians have special powers at destabilising received knowledge, questioning, for instance, whether the very concepts they use to understand the past are of themselves outdated.[4] Historians learn how to argue about these changes by means of narrative, how to join explanation with understanding, how to combine the study of the particular, the specific, and the unique with the desire to find patterns, structures, and regularities: that is, how to join what the German philosopher of the social sciences Wilhelm Windelband called the 'idiographic' and the 'nomothetic', the particularising and the generalising tendencies in the creation of knowledge that Windelband associated with the humanities and the sciences, respectively.[5] No historian would now seek laws in the records of the past but we do hope to attain some level of generality in our attempts to place events and individuals within broader patterns of culture. By combining the procedures and aspirations of both the humanities and the social sciences, history has a special (if not unique) claim to be a *critical human science*: not just as a collection of narratives or a source of affirmation for the present, but a tool of reform and a means of shaping alternative futures.

In the last generation, historians have thought a great deal about another element of their studies: space, and how to extend their work across ever greater expanses of it, beyond the nation-state that has been the default container of historical study since the nineteenth century and outward to continents, oceans, inter-regional connections, and ultimately to encompass the whole planet as part of 'world' or 'global' history. The attempt to transcend national history is now almost a cliché, as most historians question the territorial boundaries of traditional historical writing. Much more novel, and potentially even more subversive, is the move to transcend conventional periodisations, as more and more historians begin to question the arbitrary temporal constraints on their studies. *Transnational* history is all the rage. *Transtemporal* history has yet to come into vogue.[6]

Time, in all its dimensions, is the special province of the historian. 'In truth, the historian can never get away from the question of time in history: time sticks to his thinking like soil to a gardener's spade', wrote Fernand Braudel in the 1958 article in the historical journal *Annales* where he launched the term '*longue durée*'.[7] Braudel was a profound thinker about the many kinds of time – the multiple temporalities, as some might say – human beings inhabit. His aphorism captures something indispensable about the work of historians that is less central to the work of their fellow humanists and social scientists. Historians can never shake off the element of time. It clogs and drags our studies, but it also defines them. It is the soil through which we dig, the element from which history itself springs.[8]

The term *longue durée* came out of crisis, a 'general crisis of the human sciences', as Fernand Braudel put it. The nature of the crisis was in some ways familiar in light of twenty-first-century debates on the future of the humanities and social sciences: an explosion of knowledge, including a proliferation of data; a general anxiety about disciplinary boundaries; a perceived failure of cooperation between researchers in adjacent fields; and complaints about the stifling grip of an 'insidious and retrograde humanism' (*un humanisme rétrograde, insidieux*) might all have contemporary parallels. Braudel lamented that the other human sciences had overlooked the distinctive contribution of history to solving the crisis, a solution that went to the heart of the social reality that he believed was the focus of all humane inquiry: 'the opposition between the instant of time and that time which flows only slowly' (*cette opposition . . . entre l'instant et le temps lent à s'écouler*). Between these two poles lay the conventional timescales used in narrative history and by social and economic historians: spans of ten, twenty, fifty years at most. However, he argued, histories of crises and cycles along these lines obscured the deeper regularities and continuities underlying the processes of change. It was essential to move to a different temporal horizon, to a history measured in centuries or millennia: 'the history of long, even of very long duration' (*l'histoire de longue, même de très longue durée*).[9]

The ambition of Braudel and many of the historians of the *Annales* group who followed him in his quest was to find the relationship between agency and environment over the *longue durée*. This built upon a tendency visible within histories of the eighteenth and nineteenth centuries – and, indeed, long before – to presume that the work of the historian was to cover hundreds of years, or at least a few decades. In the quest to make those earlier endeavours even more rigorous, indeed falsifiable, through the acquisition of quantitative fact and the measured assessment of change, conceptions of the *longue durée* were not unchanging. For Braudel, the *longue durée* was one among a hierarchy of intersecting but not exclusive temporalities that structured all human history. He had classically described these time-scales in the Preface to his masterwork, *La Méditerranée et le Monde méditerranéen à l'époque de Philippe II* (1949), as the three histories told successively in that work: an almost unmoving one (*une histoire quasi-immobile*) of humans in their physical environment; a gently paced (*lentement rythmée*) story of states, societies, and civilisations; and a more traditional history of events (*l'histoire événementielle*), those 'brief, rapid, nervous oscillations'.[10] Appropriately, many of the features of the *longue durée* remained stable in Braudel's accounts: it was geographical, but not quite geological, time; if change was perceptible at this level, it was cyclical rather than linear; it was fundamentally static not dynamic; and it underlay all other forms of movement and activity.

Braudel ranged *l'histoire événementielle* against the *longue durée* not because such history could only treat the ephemeral – the 'froth' and 'fireflies' he notoriously disdained in *La Méditerranée* – but because it was a history too closely tied to events. In this respect, it was like the work of contemporary economists who, he charged, had harnessed their work to current affairs and to the short-term imperatives of governance.[11] Such a myopic form of historical understanding, tethered to power and focused on the present, evaded explanation, and was allergic to theory: in Braudel's view, it lacked both critical distance and intellectual substance. His solution for all the social sciences would be to go back to older models and problems, for example, to the treatment of mercantile capitalism by Marx, the 'genius' who created the first true social models on the basis of the historical *longue durée* (*vrais modèles sociaux, et à partir de la longue durée historique*). In short, even fifty years ago, Braudel himself was already recommending a return to the *longue durée*.[12]

By 1958, Braudel's increasingly adversarial relationship with the other human sciences, not least the structural anthropology of Claude Lévi-Strauss, impelled him to include a wider range of *longue-durée* structures. The term '*longue durée*' was new in historical parlance when Braudel adopted it as a term of art in his germinal article but it was not entirely novel: nineteenth-century French historians of property law had treated it over the *longue durée*, medical treatises had spoken of chronic diseases as being of long duration, sociologists studying long-term unemployment (*chômage de longue durée*) and economists tracing economic cycles were quite familiar with the phrase.[13]

Braudel's adoption of the term followed these earlier usages in tracing not the unchanging and immobile background conditions but also now the *longues durées* of culture such as Latin civilisation, geometric space, or the Aristotelian conception of the universe, which joined physical environments, enduring agricultural regimes, and the like. These were human creations that also exhibited change or rupture in moments of invention and supersession by other worldviews or traditions. They lasted longer than economic cycles, to be sure, but they were significantly shorter than the imperceptibly shifting shapes of mountains and seas, or the rhythms of nomadism and transhumance. These not quite so long *durées* could be measured in centuries and were discernible in human minds not just in natural landscapes and the human interactions with them.

Braudel admitted that his earlier reflections on the *longue durée* arose from the depressing experience of his wartime captivity in Germany in 1940–5. They were in part an attempt to escape the rhythms of camp life and to bring hope by taking a longer perspective – hence, paradoxically, his frequent use of the imagery of imprisonment in his accounts of the *longue durée*.[14] When he theorised the *longue durée* in 1958, he had come to believe that it was fundamental to any interdisciplinary understanding and that it offered the only way out of postwar presentism. His immediate motives were as much institutional as intellectual. Not long before the article appeared, Braudel had assumed both the editorship of *Annales* and the presidency of the famed VIe Section of the École Pratique des Hautes Études, both in succession to Lucien Febvre after his death in 1956. He had to justify not merely the existence but the primacy of history among the other social sciences, particularly economics and anthropology. In this competitive context, where prestige and funding were at stake as much as professional pride, he had a 'trump card ... which allowed him to claim for history the role of unifier of the human sciences in opposition to mathematics'.[15]

This agenda also dovetailed neatly with the rise in France of futurology – the forward-looking counterpart to the *longue durée* – which Braudel's friend Gaston Berger was promoting in his capacity as director general of Higher Education at the same time as he was supporting the VIe Section and engaged in creating the Maison des Sciences de l'Homme that Braudel would soon lead. On both sides of the Atlantic at this time, the future was as much an object of interest as the past and, indeed, the prospects for the two – in terms of funding, prestige and institutional viability among the human sciences – were tightly connected with each other.[16] Modern history had been forged to tell the revolutionary nation-states of nineteenth-century Europe where they were heading; in the twentieth century, modern history was being reforged to tell the world what would come after the nation disappeared.

*****

This historical orientation towards practical action and the future is hardly a recent feature of historical writing. Indeed, it has been characteristic of large swathes of the western historical tradition since classical times. The idea that history is 'philosophy teaching by examples' is ancient; the aim for history to provide pragmatic counsel to its readers is equally enduring. The Greek historian Thucydides, for example, began his history of the Peloponnesian War between the Athenians and the Spartans with the notion that his history should be useful, and that it would be useful because human nature itself was unchanging: the evidence of the past could therefore be certain to prove helpful to the future. The Roman historians may have been less convinced of the durability of human nature in a corrupted world, but their works were often political in at least two senses: that they sought to offer moral instruction to those who held official responsibility and that they were often composed by men of politics reflecting on their own action or their countrymen's in retirement or retreat from political or military office.

History in this sense was what the orator and philosopher Cicero termed *magistra vitae*: a guide to life.[17] It retained that aspiration and that authority until at least the early nineteenth century – a 2000-year period in which the past was deemed an invaluable guide to the future. And it did so not least because the Romans told long-term histories of their commonwealth (often couched in terms of moral decline) and they were followed by church historians such as Eusebius and St Augustine who told the story of the unfolding continuity of a community of faith, in Augustine's case as the story of a city paralleling Rome, the *City of God* (*Civitas Dei*) – the invisible church of all Christian believers – on its pilgrimage through a corrupting world. In the European Middle Ages, the histories of specific communities – religious, like abbeys, or secular, like towns – could be told over long stretches of time as the micro-history of a relatively small place or population extended over decades or more often centuries along the timeline of cumulative annals.[18]

What we think of as modern western historical writing began with the desire to shape the present and the future derived from classical models. The civil histories of the Renaissance and the mirrors for princes written by counsellor–historians such as Niccolò Machiavelli drew on examples from the past – often the Roman past, as in Machiavelli's *Discourses Concerning Livy* – as guides to political action in both princely and republican regimes, written either for the ruler (as Machiavelli's *Prince* was) or for citizens to digest (as Machiavelli's *Discourses* were). Many of these histories told the stories of the founding and the fortunes of particular cities and then grew to encompass early national communities and then histories of Europe, its empires, and ultimately, by the eighteenth century, the history of the whole world.

In the nineteenth century, especially in the aftermath of the French Revolution, history-writing became an increasingly important tool of political debate, with leading politicians in both France (for example, François Guizot, Adolphe Thiers, and Jean Jaurès) and Britain (Thomas Babington Macaulay and Lord John Russell, for instance) writing histories of their own revolutionary pasts to shape their national futures. It was also in this century that 'The old tradition of "pragmatic history" . . . could be refurbished to support the idea that history was useful in the education of statesmen and civil servants', even 'a school of statesmanship', in the words of Cambridge's late Victorian Regius Professor of History, J. R. Seeley.[19] Their visions of the past as advisor to future policy were accepted programmatically by the institutions of government, finance, and the military, such that history texts like Alfred Thayer Mahan's *The Influence of Sea Power upon History, 1660–1783* (1890) could become the textbook on military strategy in naval colleges in the United States, Germany, and Japan, assigned in classrooms over decades to come.[20] Out of these matrices emerged other long-range inquiries into the past: for example, the broad sweeps of the *Annales* School, and the engaged historiography of reformers across much of the twentieth century. It is to these developments that we now turn, to illustrate the rise of the *longue durée* before we describe its retreat and return in subsequent chapters.

*****

Long-term visions of the past remained bound up with policy-making and public conversations about the future, and that was a motive to go long. Like Alfred Thayer Mahan before them, historians of the 1960s and 1970s could depend upon policy-makers as an audience, and that was a rationale for staying general. Indeed, in at least one major subfield – military history – historians remain attached to the military schools and naval colleges that commission them to instruct future generals in strategy and international relations.[21] Military history remains for this reason one of the last outposts of long-term history in a short-term world.[22] Readers who care about the future may thrive on the particular detail of individual biography or battles, but generals and other strategists need the big picture on changes that take centuries to be fully expressed. It is little coincidence, then, that military writings were among the earliest sources of counterfactual thinking in the eighteenth century as strategic thinkers gamed out multiple possibilities, or that the earliest counterfactual novel in 1836 was about Napoleon and the 'conquest of the world'.[23]

Reformers and revolutionaries also need the big picture. Generation upon generation of political reformers capitalised upon history to revisit the past, some of them radicals for whom the alternatives and counterfactuals of the past gave reason for the revolutionary reconception of institutions of democracy, race, and property ownership. In a tradition that stretched back to Karl Marx, twentieth-century historians around the world continued writing about the changing nature of states, bureaucracies, and popular movements, making daring predictions about the long-term sweep of events. Economic inequality and the role of the state were the focus of one of the most ambitious attempts to look backwards and see forwards ever created. Marx's version of the history of class conflict is well known, but we have forgotten many of the historians who came after him, and who thought that the history of inequality clearly demonstrated the duty of reformers to amend government in economic systems that provided limited opportunity for the poor. For example, Sidney and Beatrice Webb, radical designers of state socialism in the late nineteenth century, turned themselves into historians in order to change the institutions around them. In eleven volumes of history on English government and its past, the husband–wife team reviewed the long history of institutions as a roadmap to future reform, demonstrating historical continuities of care of the poor and responsibility for roads from the Tudor past up to the recent present when, as they understood it, capitalism had led to the abnegation of mutual responsibility between rich and poor.[24] The books were a work of intense archival and secondary reading, still impressive enough to Gertrude Himmelfarb to make her wonder decades later 'how they had time left for meetings'. Their books formed a major strain of influence of the Fabians over political education and political movements not only in Britain but also around the world.[25]

This programme of history provided the blueprint and under-standing for a government appropriate to a changing Britain. As the Webbs understood it, the message of history was that responsibility between the classes was a constant of ethical societies, but that in every generation institutions had to be reinvented by concerned parties. Those reinventions, as they understood it, tended to take the form of cooperation between larger and larger regional entities, so that the shape of government tended to expand, first from local government to regional government, and then from regional govern-ment into national and international government, extending the benefits of democracy from isolated locales to the whole world.

The Webbs' political reasoning, like that of many of their contemporaries, was steeped in an understanding of historical change. The progressive thinking of Comte, Spencer, and Darwin suggested to them the importance of evolution over time to insti-tutions, cultures, and organisms alike, while legalist influences like Theodor Mommsen, Henry Maine, and J. F. McLennan taught them about the historical reality of irreconcilable conflict between interests warring over institutions, and the way that successive generations of reform had changed the law itself, abolishing slavery, bride kidnapping, and female infanticide.[26] Yet to these formal understandings of the influence of the past on the future, Sidney Webb added his own historical understanding of the importance of social movements and ethical awakenings, which he referred to as the 'organic changes' of political life.[27] In this view of history, knowing the past was not only useful for predicting the future; it was also a necessary precondition of making ethical decisions about how to conduct a society.

Driven by their understanding of history to pursue a better world, the Webbs' historical exercises were paired with active political life.

Both husband and wife were engaged in pamphleteering, campaign-
ing for office, and meeting with other Fabian socialists to urge on
such revolutionary programmes as the provision of clean water, free
of charge, to poor households across London. Sidney Webb sat as an
MP for Seaham, was elevated to the Lords, and served as Secretary of
State for the Colonies and Secretary of State for the Dominions in
Ramsay MacDonald's second Labour government. Perhaps most
influential was their design for the 'London Programme', that plan
for extending government to design all aspects of London's housing,
transport, and water – amenities that are today all but taken for
granted as part of the modern city.[28] It was an ethical understanding
of the city, built on a deep encounter with history, that allowed the
Webbs and their friends to convince Londoners that a city water
supply that served only the few was no way to run a town.[29]

By the twentieth century, the *longue durée* (although generally not,
of course, under that name) offered a canonical tool for writing
revisionary history in the service of reform. While the Webbs targeted
the reform of municipal and national government, their success
inspired historians with even bigger targets in mind. R. H. Tawney,
a historian of peasant experience in early-modern England, became
one of the intellectual bridges between the West and China. Having
researched the fifteenth-century struggles between export-oriented
pastoralists and sustenance-oriented poor farmers Tawney began, by
the 1920s, to consider the struggle for farmland as an international
experience of poor peasants around the globe. Armed with a deeper
understanding of economic history, he began to understand the
precedents for modern struggles against landlordism in the age of
advanced capitalism and international land reform.[30]

Indeed, Tawney's career exemplifies the activist agenda of long-
term thinking by historians of that generation. Sent to China by the
Institute of Pacific Relations in 1931, he authored an agrarian history
of China that sounded strangely similar to his histories of Britain,
wherein the drama between landlord and peasant comprised the
ultimate pivot of history and signalled the immediate need for rational
land reform.[31] In this way, history allowed Tawney's arguments, so
pertinent to the era of the People's Budget and Land Reform in Lloyd
George's Britain, to be generalised around the world. A universal
truth of class dynamics around land, narrated as a *longue-durée* history

seen through lenses ground by Marx and the American political economist and land-tax reformer Henry George, could be brought to bear on specific national traditions and its truth tested and persuasively argued for in different regions. Such applications were very different from those Braudel would later condemn among his own contemporaries for being excessively presentist, uncritical about power, and evasive about fundamental questions of causation and explanation. Long-range history was a tool for making sense of modern institutions, for rendering utopian schemes comprehensible, and for rendering revolutionary programmes for society thinkable.

The *longue durée* also appealed to those with no desire to speak to institutions, but much interest in political change. Eric Hobsbawm's many publications of the 1950s and 1960s contextualised international peasant land grabs, Marxist movements, squatters, and anarchist travellers in a long line of what he called 'primitive rebels'. The argument refuted the claim that these disorganised bands of students – whether the American Student Nonviolent Coordinating Committee or Algerian, Palestinian, or Cuban postcolonial movements – were historical failures, because they lacked a disciplined relationship with an international Marxist body. Instead, Hobsbawm showed, spontaneous popular movements demanding an extension of the enjoyment of democracy to the many and criticising the limits of capitalism had heralded revolutions since early in the modern period, coming directly out of the people's common sense rather than from any particular party or doctrine. By implication, popular movements of the postwar world should receive the same credit, whether or not they allied with an already tempered view of constitutionality, American, Soviet, or European style.[32]

Hobsbawm remained through the 1970s and 1980s a theorist of long-term political change, arguing forcefully for the liberating use of history as a set of past precedents for present change. He looked approvingly to the American Lewis Mumford and other historians of urban clearance, who were then drawing parallels between the forced evictions typical of slum clearance in the Victorian era, and modern slum clearance in the era of highway building. At the same time, he argued equally forcefully against using reductionist historical narratives for political purposes, for instance conservative movements that looked back naively to a more moral age.[33]

The use of history to advise contemporary politics exemplified by Tawney, the Webbs, and Hobsbawm was far from unique. Reformed versions of national history, offering a new vision of belonging and reform to match progressive politics, were appearing all over the world. In the United States, Charles Beard and Arthur Schlesinger, Sr pursued *longue-durée* histories of American identity, rethinking America not in terms of racial centrality but in terms of racial pluralism. The wider swathe of American historians affiliated with the project of reform and left-wing political critique includes notably the history department of the University of Wisconsin in the 1950s, where Merle Curti penned *longue-durée* histories of passive resistance, peacemaking, and democracy.[34]

In Britain, radical historians reconsidered the importance of urban planning on behalf of the poor in light of the seizures of land from the peasantry in early modern Europe. Other historians joined the modelling of government reform as inspiration for future reformers. The original sin of capitalism, as understood by historians like John and Barbara Hammond, W. G. Hoskins, Maurice Beresford, and Karl Polanyi, needed to be corrected, and their understanding of the past helped them to recommend the provision of welfare, health care, parks, and housing as necessities of life that capitalism had taken away from the poor and that government should again provide.[35]

In the postcolonial world, too, looking back to history was a natural precondition of looking forward from 1920 to 1960. New national histories, notably those of C. L. R. James and V. D. Savarkar, emerged to explain the long trajectory of thwarted rebellions that led up to national independence, and to target particular egalitarian reforms, for instance the redistribution of land, as a criterion of fulfilling this legacy. In Ghana and Delhi, even prime ministers became historians (in Trinidad and Tobago, a historian – Eric Williams – later became prime minister), as a sense of the deep past helped to orient and give confidence to those governing new nations, and to establish a sense of constitutional continuities with western traditions working alongside historical particularisms inherited from centuries of ethnic struggle.[36]

Historians were not the only ones who looked back to look forward. There were political theorists, like Hannah Arendt and Jürgen Habermas, who wove evidence gathered from the centuries into newly robust theories of democracy.[37] Lewis Mumford, the journalist of urban planning, found it necessary to refashion himself into a *longue-durée* historian in order to explain the dangers of suburban sprawl or slum clearance in the era of the interstate highway system – contemporary politics that he illuminated with the history of Victorian slum clearance and progressive movements. His macrocosmic surveys, particularly *Technics and Civilization*, included entire theories of industrialisation, mechanisation, the isolation of the working class, and time discipline that anticipated the influential theories of Michel Foucault and E. P. Thompson much later.[38]

All of these individuals looked into the past with the expectation of better understanding the future on behalf of a mass public readership and direct influence on political policy. Beard's and Schlesinger's textbooks were assigned across the United States and went into multiple editions.[39] Mumford's publications stretched into the hundreds, often in short articles in *The New Republic*, *The New Yorker*, and *Harper's Magazine*. He became one of the major figures in the American debates over race and urban clearance, denouncing the slum clearance policies of Robert Moses in New York City and providing an intellectual framework for the activism associated with Jane Jacobs.[40]

These debates made for a climate where disciplinary historians understood themselves as working in part for an audience of civil servants and social scientists who used historians' *longue-durée* perspective as material for public reform. From Tawney in the 1930s through to the 1980s, professional historians writing about land issues, in both the West and in India, entered the *longue durée* to engage this material and raise larger questions about institutional actors and public purposes. Their scholarly work constituted a conversation between disciplinary history and the institutions of international governance, ranging over centuries with the help of close readings of particular documents, events, and characters, leaning heavily on the work of other scholars in the field. For scholars who came of age in the 1950s and 1960s *longue-durée* history had been a tool for persuading bureaucrats and making policy.

Professional historians could expect an influence on policy that few historians today enjoy, whether they worked with officials or popular movements. Arthur Schlesinger, Jr worked closely on questions of policy with American president John Fitzgerald Kennedy. William Appleman Williams, author of several extensive histories of American international relations, drew from his *longue-durée* studies a critique of the dangers of America's Cold War entanglements, and shared these with the public through a series of essays urging Americans to take political action, published in *The Nation* and as separate volumes that were widely read, praised, and denounced across the academy. (He refused a post in the Kennedy administration.)[41]

The institutions of international development looked to history to supply a roadmap to freedom, independence, economic growth, and reciprocal peacemaking between the nations of the world. For example, John Boyd Orr, founding director of the Food and Agriculture Organization (FAO) of the United Nations, began his career by publishing a retrospective history of hunger that began with Julius Caesar's conquest of Britain and ended with improving relationships between farm labourers and landlords with the Agriculture Act of 1920.[42] By the 1960s, economic historians like David Landes had retooled the study of the history of the Industrial Revolution to support Green-Revolution-era development policies, promising a future of abundant riches on the back of a history of constant invention.[43] And in the 1970s, theorists of land reform like the agrarian economist Elias Tuma and the British geographer Russell King turned to *longue-durée* history, synthesising the work of historians as they consulted for the organs of international policy by contextualising present-day land reform in light of centuries of peasant struggle for participation in agrarian empire dating back to ancient Rome.[44]

There was plenty of *longue-durée* history of land policy for them to work with. As the founders of the United Nations debated appropriate interventions in the Global South to put the world on a peaceful path to world order, followers of Henry George, who were still numerous on both sides of the Atlantic, turned to the *longue durée* to offer an account of history that read landlord monopoly as the signal crime in modern history and popular ownership of land as its necessary antidote. Georgist histories appeared in the 1940s and 1950s, establishing narratives of the American agrarian tradition since Thomas Jefferson. Georgist historians laboured to make clear the tide of abuses by landlords and the necessity of populist government holding these land grabs at bay. In this vein, Alfred Noblit Chandler published his *Land Title Origins, A Tale of Force and Fraud* (1945), a history of the expanded powers of capitalists over land that traced the problem to the railway barons who were George's contemporaries and to their power over state-funded public colleges in the United States – the so-called 'land-grant' colleges funded by the Morrill Act of 1862.[45] Similarly, Aaron Sakolski published *Land Tenure and Land Taxation in America* (1957), in which he offered an intellectual history of America based on the long story of successive amendments to property law, pointing to a long history of debates over the history of ownership in land through Henry Maine, Numa Denis Fustel de Coulanges, F. W. Maitland, Paul Vinogradoff, Max Weber, and G. R. Geiger.[46] Ultimately, he reasoned, the injunctions about land were the reflection of a conception of justice, and that justice had at its core a set of spiritual and religious values where participatory access to land was the direct reflection of a doctrine that valued every human, rich and poor alike. Sakolski wrote, 'The early Christian church fathers were imbued with the ancient Hebrew traditions, and their concept of justice as related to landownership followed along the same lines'.[47] All the way back to biblical times, moral precedents could be found for challenging the accumulation of capital among landed elites, and these precedents were now packaged to promote legal action on the national and international scale.

The classical *longue durée* of social historians like Tawney, who used their sense of the deep past of institutions and movements to persuade their readers about the need for social change, was being appropriated into what might be called a 'dirty *longue durée*' in the hands of think-tanks and NGOs. In this dirty *longue durée*, non-historians dealt with an impoverished array of historical evidence to draw broad-gauge conclusions about the tendency of progress. They rarely acknowledged secondary sources or earlier traditions in thinking about the period or events in question. Typically, they dismissed Marxist or other leftist perspectives out of hand, offering an interpretation of history that vaguely coincided with free-market thinking, faith in technological progress, and the future bounty promised by western ingenuity. There are older precedents, of course, to the dirty *longue durée*, bound up with popular history in its role in popular instruction, going back at least to Charles Dupin's

Commercial Power of Great Britain (1825) and extending through the popular histories of technology of the 1850s, for example.[48]

That history can be used to promote a political bias is nothing new. Yet political and institutional conditions must align for any new genre to come into being. In the postwar United States, with the expansion of NGOs, the broadening of American hegemony and institutions of transnational governance like the United Nations and the emergence of the World Bank, the conditions were set for a wide class of consumers of *longue-durée* history, hungry for instruction about how to manage tremendous questions like famine, poverty, drought, and tyranny. As baby-boomer historians later retreated from direct engagement with these issues into the micro-history of race and class, long-term history became the domain of other writers without the historian's training – some of them demographers or economists employed by the Club of Rome or the Rand Corporation, others psychologists, biologists, self-proclaimed futurologists, or historical amateurs writing for a popular audience in the era of the alleged 'population bomb' and 'limits to growth'.[49] Dirty *longue-durée* history blossomed, but historians were not the ones with their hands in the dirt.

International governance's demand for useful historical stories incentivised the production of impossibly inclusive large-scale syntheses. The demands for historical understanding, and indeed the leaps of rationality and abstraction executed with historical data, grew larger and larger. The most fantastic of these claims were made by the physicist turned systems-theorist and futurologist, Herman Kahn, who promised to settle debates about resource use, environmental catastrophe, and consumption by examining long-term trends in world history. Kahn and his collaborators charted streamlined historical data on population growth since 8000 BCE against prophecies of future technological improvement and population control, and concluded by foreseeing a post-industrial world of 'increasing abundance'.[50]

*****

Taking these earlier examples of *longue-durée* historical writing with future-oriented intent into account, it remains to talk in more general terms about ways that thinking about our past can help us talk about our future, especially in the support of these modest purposes that we define as the public future. There is a long line of thinking about how history can help – some of it from ancient theology and political philosophy, which sought to use the examples of great lives to instruct future leaders; some of it from Marxism's dedication to using history to help the struggling masses. These traditions have a great deal to offer – an insistence on free will and the possibility that destiny is unfixed; proof of the power of counter-factual thinking to destabilise the seeming inevitability of current institutions, values, or technologies; and utopian histories about traditions that represent a better world than the one we have now.

What follows is a set of suggestions about how knowledge of history can help anyone – a member of an institution, an educated reformer, or a radical struggling to represent the voices of those traditionally excluded from power – to think with history about their options. What we offer is history where thinking about the future is no longer left to experts, be they experts in International Relations, economics, or climate science; where remaking the future is once again something within the purview of anyone who can read and talk about stories from the past. On that basis, we wish to recommend three approaches to historical thinking, in public and ethical terms, about the shaping of our shared future. Those means are a hard-headed discourse about destiny and free will, the power of counterfactual thinking, and utopian thought.

I THINKING ABOUT DESTINY AND FREE WILL

How do societies actually change their ways without collapsing? What about 'reform'? Is the amassing of raw data and abstract models the only way that individuals can use to reshape the civilisation around them? Can a civilization on a path to resource exhaustion, poisoning its own air and water, turn back and decide to divert its resources to sustainable futures for all? Or do the laws of economics portend despair for the masses and survival only for the few?

Insofar as both climate science and economics have often left us with a vision of the world in which alternative futures are scarce or non-existent, history's role must be not only to survey the data about responsibility for climate change, but also to point out the alternative

directions, the utopian byways, the alternative agricultures and patterns of consumption that have been developing all the while. As the
cultural geographer Mike Hulme puts it, in many climate debates,
'[h]umans are depicted as "dumb farmers", passively awaiting their
climate fate. The possibilities of human agency are relegated to
footnotes, the changing cultural norms and practices made invisible,
the creative potential of the human imagination ignored.'[51] Climate
change, evolutionary anthropology, and economics may well paint a
self-portrait of the species as a victim of its selfish genes, of DNA that
instructs us towards greed and exploitation no matter what, but
history and anthropology are always reminding us of the variety of
human values and forms of mutual aid.

In asking questions such as these, climate science is on the verge
of rediscovering these alternative ways of thinking about the future.
In the climate debates of the last decade, at issue has been, as the
Australian environmental historian Libby Robin argues, the notion
of 'past changes with increasing present effects'.[52] That is, climate
scientists and policy-makers have clashed over the problem of
separating out original causes that set into gear a pattern of
consequence, from primary and final causes. In order to understand
long-term change, whether of the climate or political regimes,
scholars necessarily need to understand different time-scales, actors,
periods, and events in their complex relationships with each other;
that is one of history's primary capabilities as a field. By implication,
environmental discourse is about to land squarely in the domain of
history, if indeed it has not done so already. If we really want to
understand long-term sustainability, we need to look at the past.
Thousands of civilisations before ours have questioned hierarchical
arrangements, often successfully. Knowledge of the past is therefore
a source for understanding the extent to which we have free will in
the future.

2 COUNTERFACTUAL THINKING

When we talk about sustainable economies, what we often care
about is reversibility: Could we have turned back the path to climate
change if we had banished the steam engine? Could we support
any major part of the world on a Victorian economy connected by

wind-powered vessels and efficient train-lines? Would we have to reconsider cattle farming itself to develop a sustainable agricultural ecology? How far back in time is far enough to save the planet? An index of past mistakes likewise informs the economists' question of whether economies formed around other principles than the ones that informed the twenty-first-century United States could continue to grow. Could societies like Bolivia that protect or nationalise their water supply ever compete with a free-trade world dominated by private interests? Would the super-efficient, nationalised bureaucracies of nineteenth-century civil services be able to compete with modern globalised economies? How far back would we go, if we wanted to find the origins of our current discontent, both to save our oceans and to protect the rights of poor people to food and water?

These questions are no idle speculation in the age of sustainability. Rather, scientists like geneticist Wes Jackson, whose Land Institute in Kansas has investigated principles of sustainable and responsible farming for the last three decades, have concerned themselves fastidiously with counterfactual history as the means to sketching a path forward.[53] In his reflective essays about the path to founding a sustainable agriculture, Jackson describes how mathematicians who worked with the Land Institute pored over cycles of broadening counterfactual questions about the scale of commodities networks necessary for there to be a tractor on his farm. What if there were no state-provided highways upon which to bring a bolt for the tractor? What if there were no aeroplanes with which to assemble the global board of the company that built the tractor in the first place? Would tractor-based farming still be possible in a post-carbon world?

These concerns are of immediate applicability to scientists whose stated goal is to assemble the materials for a form of farming that could feed our cities past the age of carbon crisis, into a world of rapidly changing weather, transport, and supply chains. They represent a form of inquiry with which historians are extremely familiar: counterfactual logic. Counterfactual thinking is the kind of work historians do when they speculate about what might have taken place had Napoleon not lost the battle of Waterloo, or the conditions that would have had to be in place for the First World War never to have happened. It can be a parlour game – as Voltaire mischievously asked, would the world have been different if Cleopatra's nose had been shorter? – but it informs all historical thinking about causality and, therefore, responsibility.[54] In the age of sustainability, counterfactual thinking is everyone's business. It is a form of historical logic as necessary for the inventor or entrepreneur who wants to build a climate-resistant tractor as it is for the geneticist designing farming practices for a sustainable world.

In public and in print, specialists in sustainability have unknowingly become historians. The major abstract concerns of climate scientists and the policy specialists who responded to them were questions over periodisation, events, and causality; they were problems in the philosophy of history. We are in a world that more and more looks to history to make sense of the changing nature of world events. But what if protecting the planet requires rejecting prosperity?[55] That line of thinking would require a very different theoretical toolset than the one that currently dominates corporations and policy. Moreover, a true sustainability will involve unthinking the power of terms like 'improvement', 'development', and 'growth', which modern capitalism has inherited from the last two centuries of its historic development, and which are embedded in all economists' definitions of success.[56]

Similarly, historical cases can help us pinpoint how long ago policy-makers gave up on creating a more sustainable world. Paul Thompson has traced accounts of sustainable policy-making through international consortiums of the 1980s and 1990s, zeroing in on the 1987 report of the Brundtland Commission, *Our Common Future*, as a key event that defined the position of the United States and the Global South as a 'prisoner's dilemma', where the United States could hardly be expected to act, given the indeterminacy of India's and China's positions on global climate change.[57] For policy-makers or entrepreneurs who truly want to find a way out of global gridlock, who take scientists' warnings at their words, these histories create imperative lists of the cognitive pollutants with which generations of bad policy have befouled public discourse. Without removing those impediments – discounting the 'green-washing', overcoming the 'prisoners' dilemmas', recognising that sustainability may not really be able to serve not only the planet and the people but also prosperity – there may be very little pragmatic future for climate activists.

With knowledge of these events, institutions, and discourses, however, the possible future of action becomes wider again. These stories are therefore vital for our time; they illustrate how important narrative history is for clear thinking about the future. They also raise important questions about the kind of story-telling that we most need right now.

3 UTOPIAN THINKING

Limited numbers of historians have been engaged on a project documenting these alternatives, for micro-history made the documenting of the victim under mainstream society the rule, not the documenting of alternative utopias.

The *longue-durée* utopian tradition is a rich one. Lewis Mumford's *The Story of Utopias* (1922) narrated the history of utopian thinking from Sir Thomas More to nineteenth-century fantasy writer H. Rider Haggard, and the tradition can be traced even further back, to Plato, and forward to much of contemporary science fiction. These texts, from the sober to the absurd, Mumford argued, pointed not least to the primary source of thinking about the reform of cities, and one of the major intellectual sources to contribute to the rise of urban planning in the late nineteenth century.[58] Later, Wes Jackson's *New Roots for Agriculture* (1980) articulated a tradition from the ancient world through the transcendentalists and modern soil science warning about the consequences of agriculture out of touch with natural cycles, mapping upon those failures the rise of new agricultural practices around factory farming and top-down management, and documenting the rise of an alternative movement of organic farming.[59] These stories bring up to date institutional struggles about how societies confront ecological problems: they bring climate change down from the spectre of an incontrovertible force making war upon our selfish genes, irreconcilable with the structure of our DNA itself, and put climate change and sustainability back in the realm of human institutions, which can be faced in terms of social and political reform.

Thus in our time, the possibility of conceiving of a reform tradition is of vital importance for sustained engagement with agriculture and climate change at any level other than that of professional economics or climate science. For scientists in the 1980s and 1990s who wished to rethink the consequences of the Green Revolution, new *longue-durée* histories of patriarchy and ecology coming out of the history of science were of immense inspiration; centuries-long revision of the tradition of Francis Bacon up to factory farming reverberates through the works of dissident scientists who have come to represent important voices in thinking through a future built around organic farming. More recently, a revival of the utopian tradition in *longue-durée* history has pointed to the rise of state-sponsored research on permaculture in Australia, where constraints over water made alternative agriculture a focused subject of legislation and research from above already by the 1930s.[60] Those alternatives, first blooming thirty years ago, have today proliferated into a rich set of science and alternative institutions to support intensive, sustainable small farming of a kind that could be reproduced, with proper adaptation to local conditions and institutions, across the globe.

Some of the stories that give grist to the mill of alternative agriculture are built out of a series of short excavations in the archives of industrial agriculture and national governments. But many more trace a history of ideas over generations, proving to contemporary activists that their dissident views in fact represent a long tradition of contestation. *Longue-durée* histories of local farming that suggest the threats and risks characteristic of other places and times are easy to come by. Other *longue-durée* research into alternative forms of capitalism includes the remarkable story of the world worker–cooperative movement, its successes and suppression in foreign policy, again a *longue-durée* history which ends up highlighting forgotten varieties of capitalism as possible viable alternatives for a more democratic and sustainable future for our own time.[61] Those proliferating pasts and alternative societies point us to a horizon of alternative and proliferating possible futures. In conversations such as these, history speaks to economics and climate science about the diversity of past responses and future possibilities. In the context of a deep past, conversations about a deep future may once again become possible. To know how they might be possible – and what resistance they might face – we need to know more about the retreat of the *longue durée* among historians in the late twentieth century.

*****

Long-term argumentation is a very different mode of engagement with stories than is a long-term survey. The inquiry has to be scaled over the length of that set of developments, rather than taking one diagnostic slice, as has tended to happen in the world of the micro-history. We need a careful examination of these events, building upon existing micro-historical studies towards the pinpointing of particular turning-points and watersheds in history, moments of revolution that destabilised institutions, climates, and societies. This long-term history needs to benefit from micro-history's refinement of the exemplary particular, those short moments in history during which the structures of power, hierarchy, and imagination are revealed.

This process of temporal refinement has been under way for some time, however. Many history professors find themselves at some point in the business of constructing long-term surveys of time in the form of our syllabi. In departments of History, these surveys have names like 'World Civilization' or 'American History, 1760–1865'. In the form of books, surveys often take the form of disjointed chapter-length examinations of discrete periods that have little to do with one another. But there is such a thing as understanding these turning points afresh. Already in 1987, William H. McNeill proposed that the major turning-point of globalisation happened around 1000 CE, when new trade routes coalesced into a deeper pattern of exchange.[62] In the decades since then, world historians have been comparing and analysing nuanced dates for establishing histories not only of globalisation, but also of racialised thinking and racism, of class consciousness, of peacemaking, and of democracy, to name but a few.[63] All of these refinements to our understanding of watershed moments are built upon a deep foundation of micro-historical research.

Indeed, the number and variation of turning-points and eras that historians have proposed suggest, as Jürgen Osterhammel conjectures, that 'the sense of epochs has been steadily weakening'.[64] The horizontal chronology of one age following the next is being succeeded, in terms of how we think about time, by a topological flow of 'multiple modernities', intersecting and weaving, in which the forces of causation, according to Manuel De Landa, may be conceptualised as different elements – rock, water, and air – all changing, but some changing faster than the others.[65] The challenge that history faces, insofar as history is the natural arbiter of big-picture stories about time, is to rewrite the histories of climate and inequality, the very stories that give our civilisation nightmares, in terms of a comprehensible knowledge grounded in data and described by overlapping flows of materiality, construct, and cause.

Stories with a long-term argument can have the powerful effect of banishing myths and overturning false laws. This, and not the mere appreciation of antiquities, is the reason that universities have history departments and the reason for history's classical mission as *magistra vitae*, the teacher of all aspects of life. We must use the past in the indispensable work of turning out the falsehoods established in the past, of making room for the present and the future, lest those mythologies come to dominate our policy-making and our relationships.

Longue-durée history allows us to step outside of the confines of national history to ask about the rise of long-term complexes, over many decades, centuries, or even millennia: only by scaling our inquiries over such durations can we explain and understand the genesis of contemporary global discontents. What we think of as 'global' is often the sum of local problems perceived as part of a more universal crisis, but the fact of aggregation – the perception that local crises are now so often seen as instances of larger structural problems in political economy or governance, for example – is itself a symptom of the move towards larger spatial scales for understanding contemporary challenges. Those challenges need to be considered over longer temporal reaches as well. In this regard, the *longue durée* has an ethical purpose. It proposes an engaged academia trying to come to terms with the knowledge production that characterises our own moment of crisis, not just within the humanities but across the global system as a whole.

CHAPTER 2

The short past: or, the retreat of the longue durée

A history undergraduate places aside her work on an assignment for a few hours to surf the Web, and what she sees there worries her. It always troubles her, because her conscience keeps asking her how to connect her work with the world outside the university. She thinks of herself as a reformer, and corruption, pollution, and inequality rock her sense of justice. What can she do to learn about the levers of change, to talk to the public about how they work, to develop a cadre of students trained to think about such things? The answers that her teachers give can be summed up in one disappointing word: focus. Focus her questions; focus on her archival sources. University training, she will hear in many of her courses, is about developing professional expertise in analysing evidence, not answering the big questions. While sophistication with data about the past is well and good for learning to ask precise, academic questions and how to answer them, sometimes our student wonders when and how the big questions can be asked, and by whom.

Students at Oxford in the late 1960s were having a very different experience of historical questions and their relevance. They read news reports of union strikes in Paris where students showed up in solidarity. They read about sexual revolution and the largest migration in American history, converging on encampments in San Francisco where experiments in property ownership, psychedelic drugs, and communal living were under way. All the while, *longue-durée* historians like Eric Hobsbawm were publishing histories of resistance that contextualised May 1968 in the centuries that preceded it. This episode was not without context, they argued. Rather, centuries of struggle by slaves, working people, and women had preceded and conditioned many of the political movements now voicing their demands in public.[1] So while many of the college students reading about Paris or the Prague Spring went to join them, some radicals chose another path, and went in search of history.

The future historian of Germany, Geoff Eley, was one of these students, 'a young person seeking change in the world', as he tells us in the first line of his memoir.[2] Like many history undergraduates at the time, the best way to understand the warrant and potential of these incipient movements was to understand them against the background of long-term political change. There were few questions in his mind as to whether the public needed thinkers about long-term change: change was everywhere around them. For students reading Tawney and Hobsbawm by day and watching revolution on the television in the evening, history's imminence was incontrovertible. For this generation, thinking about the future almost automatically evoked the resource of looking at the past. However one chose to think about that history, there was no question about narrowing one's mind or one's ambition.

The way that Eley chose to answer big questions when he trained as a professional historian at the University of Sussex in the early 1970s was to focus his vision and narrow his sources. His doctoral thesis treated sixteen years of German naval history and his first articles covered ten or twenty years at a time, as he delved into the archives about the small elite of Germans affiliated with the military who helped to propel their nation to nationalism in the decades leading up to the Third Reich. He pillaged the Freiburg community archive and its military archive for their correspondence, for how they spoke about their political organising, the nation, the people, and foreign policy.[3] Eley and most of his generation mastered one archive at a time and worked with the conviction that these intense excursions into the history of the 'Short Past' could illuminate the politics of the immediate present.

In the decades since 1968, focusing on narrow time-scales like this has come to dominate most university training in history. It determines how we write our studies, where we look for sources, and which debates we engage. It also determines where we break off the conversation. Yet no revolution comes without a price. The transition to the Short Past meant that fewer and fewer students trained on the long-term perspective that characterised Eric

Hobsbawm, for example, who stood out for his willingness to span centuries as well as continents. Whether undergraduates, graduate students, or faculty, most people who work with data about time have been trained to examine the past on the scale of an individual life, not the trans-generational perspective on the rise and fall of institutions that characterised the *longue durée*. As students in classrooms were told to narrow and to focus, the professionals who deal with past and future began to restrict not only their sources and their data, but sometimes also their ideas.

The examples in this chapter have mostly been drawn from the English-speaking world but we believe that the argument here, as throughout this book, has relevance for historians more generally at a time when short-term horizons constrict the views of most of our institutions. In some fields, broad historical time-scales never went away: for example, in historical sociology or in world-systems theory.[4] However, in the field of history, the *longue durée* – associated, as we have seen, with Fernand Braudel and the French *Annales* school of historians, but soon more widely diffused – flourished and then withered away. What replaced it – the view of the Short Past – often had its own radical mission, one of changing the world, but it also had its own limitations.

*****

The historians who came of age around 1968 had a very different approach to the past than did those of the *longue durée* a generation before. As students and writers about history, as thinkers and public intellectuals, this generation found more material in short-term history than, perhaps, any generation before it. Obscure archives of workers' trade unions in the south of France or the north of England allowed them to look at the micro-dynamics between rank-and-file workers and leaders, to ask questions about how and when group decision-making is possible, and when and how a small group of organised individuals can overturn an entire outmoded system of privilege and production. In narrowing, they found the freedom to take on big ideas and to publish authoritative and insightful perspectives that helped the public to contextualise enormous forces like racism or nationalism as constructed developments rather than as a natural social order some-how predestined to shape human minds for eternity.

The micro-historical perspective of the Short Past helped a historian like Geoff Eley to reflect on politics more broadly, which he did for the profession in *The Peculiarities of German History* (1984), a precocious and path-breaking co-authored attack on the enduring myth of Germany's inevitable *Sonderweg*.[5] Sometimes his history was written for the public, published in organs like the *London Review of Books*, where he helped to keep a discussion of the Holocaust alive and pertinent to the racism that rocked Thatcherite Britain in the years of the Brixton Riots.[6] Eley and his cohort were part of a university that believed in using the disciplines, including the humanities, as a tool for rethinking civil society and international order on enormous time-scales. While Eley did his graduate training at the University of Sussex, whose red-brick modernism still bespoke of futurism, colleagues there in anthropology, sociology, and economics were working to advise the United Nations and World Bank about the future of housing and democracy. They were using recent work in the history of technology to reconceptualise programmes of international aid and economic development. They believed in overturning the old order of nations, rethinking the future of India and Africa in the wake of empire, and using technology and democracy to lift up all.[7] On campuses such as these, it was still clear that looking to the past was a source of ample material for thinking about futures on a global scale.

It is to this generation, with their ambitions for changing the world, that we owe the strength of the commandment to focus on the past in order to gain insight into the present. In the era when Geoff Eley was learning his trade, the Short Past was committed to public discourse and changing the world, deeply intertwined with riot, revolution, and reform. These ties between historians and social movements were well established in the generation of Sidney and Beatrice Webb and R. H. Tawney, down to the 1960s and 1970s, when American diplomatic historian William Appleman Williams worked with the NAACP in a small town on the Texas coast, and historian of the working class E. P. Thompson delivered sermons to peace rallies in London before going on to help found a major European movement for nuclear disarmament.[8] In the 1970s, Hobsbawm's own attention turned from revolution to the history of invented traditions, allowing him to contextualise the celebration of the ancient battle site of Masada in the new state of Israel alongside other invented traditions, from Nazi Germany to the nation of Ghana to the Mexican Revolution.[9] Even as the class of 1968 came of age, the senior historians around them were continuing to respond, often intimately, to political events and social conditions of the present, using the past to make sense of the present. Using the past to look backwards in time and developing firm opinions about the future as a result was nothing new. But in the 1970s, political movements could take on an Oedipal cast.

Young people coming of age in the 1970s entered a political ecosystem that increasingly was bent upon rejecting the institutional ties typical of an earlier generation. In the United States of the Vietnam War, ties with the institutions of rule were proof of the corruption of the older generation, according to anarchist Paul Goodman, one of the inspirations of many a student movement. According to Goodman, 'the professors' had given up their 'citizenly independence and freedom of criticism in order to be servants of the public and friends of the cops'.[10] True rebellion had to reject its ties to policy.

Young historians saw themselves as rebels. According to Eley, the cultural turn was a kind of personal liberation for younger historians who 'bridl[ed] against the dry and disembodied work of so much conventional historiography', for whom theory 'resuscitated the archive's epistemological life'. The rebellion of young historians against old here parallels, in terms of rhetoric, the anti-war, free-speech, and anti-racism youth movements of the same moment in the late 1960s and 1970s: it reflected a call of conscience, a determination to make the institution of history align with a more critical politics. Talking about the 'big implications' of this reaction, Eley is direct: historians of his generation took their politics in the form of a break with the corrupted organs of international rule, those very ones that had been the major consumers of *longue-durée* history for generations before.[11]

In 1970, the Short Past had another, practical advantage over *longue-durée* thought: it helped individuals to face the professional and economic realities of the academic job market with something new up their sleeves. A generation with limited prospects on the job market increasingly defined itself by its mastery of discrete archives.

As young historians simultaneously infused their archival visits with the politics of protest and identity that formed so vast a part of its milieu, anglophone historians widely adopted the genre of the Short Past; the result was the production of historical monographs of exceptional sophistication.

In the United States, state subsidies for the education of returning soldiers under the GI Bill of 1944 had led to an explosion of postwar graduate programmes in all fields, including History. The training time for the PhD was expanded from three to six years, and often extended even beyond that. By the late 1970s, when a new generation of American graduate students came of age in a professionalised university setting, 'the academic labor market in most fields became saturated, and there was concern about overproduction of Ph.D.s', reported the National Science Foundation: 'The annual number of doctorates awarded rose from 8,611 in 1957 to 33,755 in 1973, an increase of nearly 9 percent per year'.[12] Insufficient numbers of jobs were created to harbour all of those PhDs, however, and graduates of history programmes increasingly looked to distinguish themselves from their peers through innovative approaches to archives. In the earliest years of doctoral training in the American historical profession, a thesis could cover two centuries or more, as had Frederick Jackson Turner's study of trading-posts across North American history or W. E. B. Du Bois' work on the suppression of the African slave-trade, 1638–1870.[13] A 2013 survey of some 8,000 history dissertations written in the United States since the 1880s showed that the average period covered in 1900 was about seventy-five years; by 1975, that had fallen to about thirty years. Only in the twenty-first century did it rebound to between seventy-five and a hundred years (see Figure 2).[14]

There were parallels on the other side of the Atlantic. Eley's memoir of his years on the tightening job market recalls how he found himself fighting alongside his peers for their professional positions. The major weapon used in this battle was an attention to local detail, a practice derived from the urban history tradition, where German and British city histories frequently narrated labour altercation as part of the story of urban community. Indeed, the increasing emphasis on the extremely local experiences in the work of historians such as Gareth Stedman Jones and David Roediger

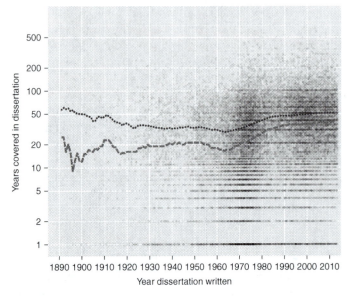

Figure 2 Number of years covered in History dissertations in the United States,
c. 1885–2012. *Note*: Median time covered = dashed line, mean length of time
covered = dotted line; dots represent the use of a year in a dissertation title.
Source: Benjamin Schmidt, 'What Years Do Historians Write About?',
Sapping Attention (9 May 2013).

allowed exactly such an examination of race, class, and power in the
community that allowed the historian to reckon as contingent the
failures of working-class movements to transform the nation.[15]
Exploiting archives became a coming-of-age ritual for a historian,
one of the primary signs by which one identified disciplined commitment to methodology, theoretical sophistication, a saturation in
historiographical context, and a familiarity with documents. Gaining
access to a hitherto unexploited repository signalled that one knew
the literature well enough to identify the gaps within it, and that one
had at hand all of the tools of historical analysis to make sense of any
historiographical record, no matter how obscure or how complex the
identity of its authors. Every historian was encouraged to get a taste
for the archives: not to get one's hands dirty was hardly to be a
historian at all.[16]

As historians of the Short Past began to rethink their relationship to archives and audiences, archival mastery became the index of specialisation and temporal focus became ever more necessary. With a few exceptions, the classic works of the 1970s, 1980s, and 1990s concentrated on a particular episode: the identification of a particular disorder within psychology, or the analysis of a particular riot in the labour movement, for instance.[17] Almost every social historian experimented in some sense with short-*durée* historical writing to engage with specific forms of institution-making, each filling in a single episode in the long story of labour, medicine, gender, or domesticity. The cases of psychological diagnoses followed a particular model, each study's periodisation constrained to coincide with the life of the doctors involved with original work – the diagnosis of hysteria, the fad of mesmerism, or the birth of agoraphobia, or Ian Hacking's discourse in *Mad Travelers* (1998) on fugue states which departed from a twenty-year medical tradition suddenly deprived of its 'ecological niche'.[18]

Biological time-scales of between five and fifty years became the model for field-breaking work in history. The micro-historians revolutionised historical writing about unions and racism, the nature of whiteness, and the production of history itself. Indeed, a flood of doctoral dissertations since that time has concentrated on the local and the specific as an arena in which the historian can exercise her skills of biography, archival reading, and periodisation within the petri-dish of a handful of years. In the age of the Short Past, doctoral supervisors often urged young historians to narrow, not to broaden, their focus on place and time, trusting that serious work on gender, race, and class comes most faithfully out of the smallest, not the largest, picture. Yet, according to Eley, the project of politically engaged social history was largely a failure, due precisely to this over-concentration on the local: 'With time, the closeness and reciprocity ... between the macro-historical interest in capturing the direction of change within a whole society and the microhistories of particular places – pulled apart'. Eley even contrasted local social history with another politically oriented history, that from the *Annales* tradition, which much like his own project promised a 'total' critique of history of the present.[19]

The Short Past produced the fundamentalist school of narrowing time horizons called 'micro-history'. Micro-history largely abandoned grand narrative or moral instruction in favour of focus on a particular event: for example, the shame-inducing charivaris of early modern France analysed by Natalie Zemon Davis or the mystifying cat massacres of eighteenth-century Paris unpacked by Robert Darnton.[20] Micro-history had originated in Italy as a method for testing *longue-durée* questions, in reaction to the totalising theories of Marxism and the *Annales* School. Its quarry was what Edoardo Grendi famously called the 'exceptionally "normal"' (*eccezionalmente normale*) and its aim was to articulate different scales of analysis simultaneously.[21] Its method was therefore not incompatible with temporal depth, as in a work such as Carlo Ginzburg's study of the *benandanti* and the witches' sabbath, which moved between historical scales of days and of millennia.[22] Nor was micro-history originally disengaged from larger political and social questions beyond the academy: its Italian roots included a belief in the transformative capacity of individual action 'beyond, but not outside, the constraints of prescriptive and oppressive normative systems'.[23] However, when transposed to the anglophone historical profession, the Short Past produced a habit of writing that depended upon shorter and shorter time-scales and more and more intensive use of archives. In some sense, the more obscure or difficult to understand a particular set of documents, the better: the more that a strange archive tested the writer's sophistication within a wealth of competing theories of identity, sexuality, professionalism, and agency, the more the use of the archive proved the scholar's fluency with sources and commitment to immersion in the field. A suspicion towards grand narratives also fuelled a movement towards empathetic stories of past individuals with whom even non-professional readers could identify; such 'sentimentalist' accounts risked the charge of 'embracing the local and personal at the expense of engagement with larger public and political issues' even as they often earned their authors fame and popularity within and beyond the academy.[24]

Later generations would take the time horizons of the Short Past as a matter of course. To get a job as a historian, one needed to engage in an innovative reading of the past, and the Short Past lent weight to numerous new interpretations and internecine arguments. The generation of 1968 landed in the middle of an already ongoing social turn, a revolution in looking at history 'from the bottom up' and away from the history of elites to the experiences of ordinary people, the subaltern, the marginalised, and the oppressed. Then there was the linguistic turn – a movement adopted from analytic philosophy which historians adapted to their own purposes to reveal the construction of the world and social experience through language and concepts.[25] The linguistic turn led to a cultural turn and to a broader revival of cultural history.[26] Since then, there has been a series of turns away from national history, among them variously the transnational turn, the imperial turn, and the global turn.[27] The authors of this book have both been guilty of promoting the language of turns: one of us recently offered a genealogy of the 'spatial turn' across the disciplines generally; the other has surveyed the prospects for an 'international turn' in intellectual history more specifically.[28] To speak of scholarly movements as 'turns' implies that historians always travel along a one-lane highway to the future, even if that road is circuitous with many twists and bends to it. For that very reason, some questioning of turns is in order, along with a readiness to consider the value of *returns*, such as the return of the *longue durée*.

So frequent and so unsettling is all the talk about turns that in 2012 the *American Historical Review* – the anglophone historical profession's leading journal – convened a major forum on 'Historiographic "Turns" in Critical Perspective' to survey the phenomenon.[29] So-called 'critical turns' have reassured professional historians that we are indeed inspecting our sources and our questions afresh. But as the *American Historical Review* authors pointed out, even critical turns can become banal. They can mask old patterns of thought that have become entrenched. However large our questions, however they have documented the construction of yet another facet of human experience – the spatial, the temporal, or the emotional – the answers of history still tended, until recently, to be marked with the common imprint: the narrow, intense focus of the Short Past.

The Short Past was not confined to social history, or indeed to the American historical profession. At around the same moment, in Cambridge, Quentin Skinner was leading a charge among intellectual historians against various long-range tendencies in the field – most notably, Arthur Lovejoy's diachronic history of ideas and the canonical approach to 'Great Books' by which political theory was generally taught – in favour of ever tighter rhetorical and temporal contextualisation. This has been read as a reaction to the collapse of grand narratives in postwar Britain, notably the retreat of empire and the collapse of Christianity: 'Focusing on context ensured a more accurate scholarship, while attempting to stay clear of any political mythology, old or new.'[30] The contextualism of the so-called Cambridge School focused almost exclusively on the synchronic and the short-term settings for arguments treated as moves in precisely orchestrated language-games or as specific speech-acts, not as instantiations of timeless ideas or enduring concepts.

The contextualists' original enemies were the Whigs, Marx, Namier, and Lovejoy, but their efforts were construed as an assault on anachronism, abstraction, and grand theory more generally. Yet Skinner's own effort in 1985 to promote 'the return of grand theory' in the human sciences was beset by the paradox that many of the thinkers who inspired or represented this revanche – among them, Wittgenstein, Kuhn, Foucault, and Feyerabend – expressed 'a willingness to emphasize the local and the contingent ... and a correspondingly strong dislike ... of all overarching theories and singular schemes of explanation'. Reports of the return of grand theory seemed exaggerated in the 1980s: far from returning, it was retreating into the twilight like Minerva's owl.[31] It was not until the late 1990s that Skinner himself returned to longer-range studies – of Thomas Hobbes in a tradition of rhetoric extending back to Cicero and Quintilian; of neo-Roman theories of liberty derived from the *Digest* of Roman law; and of conceptions of republicanism, the state, and freedom in post-medieval history – that foreshadowed a broader return to the *longue durée* among intellectual historians.[32]

From the late 1970s onwards, broad swathes of the historical profession had entered a period of retreat into short-*durée* studies across multiple domains, from social history to intellectual history, nearly simultaneously. Tension between the historian's arts of *longue-durée* synthesis and documentary history or biography is nothing new. Shorter time-scales had, of course, a literary place before they influenced the writing of professional history. From Plutarch's parallel *Lives of the Noble Greeks* and Romans to Samuel Smiles' *Lives of the Engineers* (1874–99), biography had formed an instructive moral substrate to the writing of history, often focusing on a purportedly diachronic category of 'character' visible in these exemplary life-stories.[33] An emphasis on short-term history also erupted wherever history was called in to help decide between long-term visions in conflict with each other. According to Lord Acton, the acquisition of documents and the turning over of church and local archives by Michelet, Mackintosh, Bucholtz, and Migne were bound up with a desire to settle the legacy of the French Revolution, whether to understand it as 'an alien episode' and rebellion against natural authority or instead as 'the ripened fruit of all history'.[34] A revolution in documents resulted, where the historian's role changed from narrative artist and synthesiser to politic critic settling controversial debates with the power of exact readings of precise documents. Institutional history, in this role, took up the task of interpreting the liberal tradition, worked out through such targeted studies of pivotal moments as Elie Halévy's *L'Angleterre en 1815* (1913). Short-term histories often focused on journalistic exposition, particular controversies, and disputed periods, for example, the poet Robert Graves' *The Long Week-End* (1940), a meditation on the fading utopianism present at the beginning of the First World War revisited from the perspective of distance at the start of a second war.[35]

Anxiety about specialisation – about 'knowing more and more about less and less' – had long dogged the rise of professionalisation and expertise, initially in the sciences but then more broadly, since the 1920s (see Figure 3). Three decades later, the British novelist Kingsley Amis acutely satirised the constraints professionalisation placed on younger historians in his *Lucky Jim* (1953). The title character, a hapless junior lecturer in a provincial university named Jim Dixon, frets throughout the novel about the fate of the article

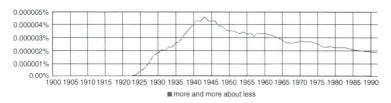

Figure 3 Usage of 'more and more about less [and less]', 1900–90
Source: Google Ngram viewer.

that is meant to win him his professional spurs. The subject is 'The Economic Influence of the Developments in Shipbuilding Techniques, 1450 to 1485', a topic the narrator mercilessly skewers. 'It was a perfect title', the narrator notes, 'in that it crystallized the article's niggling mindlessness, its funereal parade of yawn-enforcing facts, the pseudo-light it threw upon non-problems'. Yet, within only a few years of *Lucky Jim*'s publication, a conscientious supervisor might have discouraged an essay on such an absurdly ambitious and wide-ranging theme.[36]

Yet never before the 1970s had an entire generation of professional historians made so pronounced a revolt against *longue-durée* thinking, as scholars born during the baby-boom rejected a style of writing typical of relevant, engaged historians in the generation just before their own. The works of Marxist historians, from E. P. Thompson's *The Making of the English Working Class* (1963) to Eugene Genovese's *Roll, Jordan, Roll* (1974), borrowed techniques from the study of folklore like the examination of ballads, jokes, and figures of speech in order to characterise working-class and slave culture and the widespread attitudinal tensions between subaltern and elite.[37] That willingness to characterise grand moments shifted in the early 1970s in the work of social historians of labour like Joan Wallach Scott and William Sewell, whose work focused upon a single factory floor or patterns of interaction in a neighbourhood, and imported from sociology habits of attention to individual actors and details.[38] To be sure, the focused attention of these historians was not necessarily in conflict with broader perspectives: Sewell's study of work and revolution in France spanned decades 'from the Old Regime to 1848'. Nor could micro-historians operate without a *longue-durée* framework for their thinking. Rather than writing their own long versions of history, however, historians of the Short Past tended to outsource it to German and French social theorists of the 1960s and 1970s. Michel Foucault's centuries-long histories of sexuality, discipline, prisons, and government order offered a long-term framework sceptical of institutional progress for many a historian of fertility, education, welfare, and statistics in the Short Past, while Jürgen Habermas' optimistic account of eighteenth-century public life offered an alternative framework.[39] The prison and the coffeehouse became the two poles of macro-history, the pessimistic and the optimistic account of modern institutions, into which micro-historians of the Short Past poured their finer-grained details. Whether cited or not, these theories oriented many a detailed history of the Short Past in history, historical sociology, and historical geography.[40] From 1968 to approximately 2000, many a researcher in those disciplines was thus temporarily relieved of the obligation of original thinking about the past and its significance for the future. The task of understanding shifted from generalisations about the aggregate to micro-politics and the successes or failures of particular battles within the larger class struggles.

*****

In the decades since 1968, the Short Past has come to dominate training in thinking about time in the university. Modern textbooks geared to teach historians how to do research – at least, those published in the United States – have concentrated on the impor-tance of narrowing questions to the specificities of the time-period. For example, Florence N. McCoy's classic American textbook for budding historians from 1974 followed a student's process for choos-ing a research paper topic. In the end, the student narrows down her topic from wanting to study Oliver Cromwell (a topic too broad for McCoy) to researching Cromwell on the union of Scotland with England. In this vision of university education, the latter topic is more appropriate than the former because it teaches the student to emulate the specialisation of a society run by experts, each of whom competes in terms of narrowness with others in their field. The paper topic on Cromwell and Anglo-Scottish union is well suited to this lesson in keeping one's head down, because the topic 'provides an opportunity to learn something that only the specialist in Anglo-Scots diplomatic relations knows'.[41]

The prejudices of the field changed alongside training. Up to the 1970s, it had been routine for historians to critique each other's work in terms of the possible irrelevance of a subject looked at too narrowly. Those charges of narrowness were again and again levelled against young historians into the 1960s and 1970s. When they turned to periods of as little as fifty years, reviewers were wont to react. A reviewer of Paul Bew's *Land and the National Question in Ireland, 1858–82* (1979) was unimpressed to discover that the book actually confined itself to the three years between 1879 and 1882, even while he congratulated the author for his detailed study of living standards and material expectations.[42] Even grand sweeps of history could be chided, when their title and introduction seemed to promise more. When Rodney Barker published a history of what he called 'modern Britain' but only addressed a century, his 1979 reviewer mocked him for only covering the period from 1880 to 1975, accusing the author of covering 'too short a period'.[43]

But by 1979, times were changing, and the charge of 'too short' was not so much of a scandal. When in 1933, Arthur Schlesinger, Sr, published his history of American racial pluralism, *The Rise of the City, 1878–98*, the work on two decades was itself part of an ambitious multi-volume, multiple-authored attempt to chart the trajectory of America since its beginning. His introduction gave a sweeping overview of cities in Persia and Rome, but Schlesinger's research turned upon the patterns of migration and immigration that characterised two decades around the time of his own birth. Appalled by the narrowness of temporal focus, Schlesinger's fellow historian Carl Becker of Cornell accused him of slicing up history into periods too short to learn from. In the expanding university of the 1960s and 1970s, data were becoming more important, and Schlesinger had been elevated to canonical status. By 1965, when Schlesinger died, his Harvard colleagues were counter-accusing Becker of 'making sweeping generalizations over long spans of history'. The official charge of failure had changed from 'too short' to 'too long'.[44]

As the Short Past became the rule, historians increasingly ignored the art of relating deep time to the future. At least in the English-speaking world, micro-historians rarely took the pains to contextualise their short time horizons for a common reader; they were playing in a game that rewarded intensive subdivision of knowledge. In a university more intensively committed to the division of labour, there was ever less room for younger researchers to write tracts aimed at a general audience or for the deep temporal perspective which such writing often required. This was of a part with a more general retreat from grand narratives in what the American intellectual historian Daniel Rodgers has called an 'Age of Fracture' defined centrally by the contraction of temporal horizons: 'In the middle of the twentieth century, history's massive, inescapable, larger-than-life presence had weighed down social discourse. To talk seriously was to talk of the long, large-scale movements of time.' By the 1980s, modernisation theory, Marxism, 'theories of long-term economic development and cultural lag, the inexorabilities of the business cycle and the historians' *longue durée*', had all been replaced by a foreshortened sense of time focused on one brief moment: the here and now of the immediate present.[45]

In the 1980s, historians on both sides of the Atlantic began to complain that specialisation had created acute fragmentation in their field. 'Historical inquiries are ramifying in a hundred directions at once, and there is no coordination among them . . . synthesis into a coherent whole, even for limited regions, seems almost impossible', the Americanist Bernard Bailyn observed in his 1981 Presidential address to the American Historical Association (AHA). 'The Challenge of Modern Historiography', as he called it, was precisely 'to bring order into large areas of history and thus to reintroduce . . . [it] to a wider reading public, through synthetic works, narrative in structure, on major themes'.[46] Shortly afterwards, in 1985, another former AHA President, the *longue-durée* historian of the age of the democratic revolution, R. R. Palmer, complained of his own field of French history, 'Specialization has become extreme . . . it is hard to see what such specialization contributes to the education of the young or the enlightenment of the public'.[47] And in 1987 the young British historian David Cannadine similarly condemned the 'cult of professionalism' that meant 'more and more academic historians were writing more and more academic history that fewer and fewer people were actually reading'. The result, Cannadine warned, 'was that all too often, the role of the historian as public teacher was effectively destroyed'.[48] Professionalisation had led to marginalisation. Historians were increasingly cut off from non-specialist readers as they talked only to one another about ever narrower topics studied on ever shorter time-scales.

Peter Novick, in his moralising biography of the American historical profession, *That Noble Dream* (1988), saw the 1980s as the moment when it became clear that fragmentation was endemic and 'there was no king in Israel'. The anthropological turn, with its emphasis on 'thick description'; the export of micro-history from Italy via France; the destabilisation of the liberal subject by identity politics and postcolonial theory; the emergent scepticism with regard to grand narratives diagnosed by Jean-François Lyotard: these were all centrifugal forces tearing the fabric of history apart.[49] Yet jeremiads like those from Bailyn, Palmer, Cannadine, and Novick may have missed the central point: the disintegration of the profession was parasymptomatic of a larger trend, the triumph of the short *durée*.

The combination of archival mastery, micro-history, and an emphasis on contingency and context, powered by a suspicion of grand narratives, a hostility to whiggish teleologies, and an ever-advancing anti-essentialism, determined an increasing focus on the synchronic and the short-term across wide swathes of the historical profession. The stress on case-studies, individual actors, and specific speech-acts gradually displaced the long-run models of Braudel, Namier, Mumford, Lovejoy, and Wallerstein with the micro-history of Darnton, Davis, and others. Barely a decade ago, a French historian of America noted dyspeptically, '[a]n approach in terms of *longue durée* might seem old-fashioned today when postmodernism pushes scholars towards fragmented and fugacious inquiries, but it remains an asymptotic ideal we may tend toward, without being able to reach it some day'.[50] However, as the founders of *micro-history* well understood, a history that surprises us necessarily must depend upon a critical reading of data, and often the inspection of data of many different sorts. Critical history of this kind has a public purpose to serve, one that means synthesising available data from many sources and debunking the now-flourishing illusions about our collective past and its meaning. But the Short Past needs to recover some of the forms of commitment to big questions that helped to bring it into being in 1968.

In this age of global warming and coming wars over land and water, histories of class struggles over resources and their distribution, within societies and among them, are needed now more than ever. In the last forty years, the public has embraced a series of proliferating myths about our long-term past and its meaning for the future, almost none of them formulated by professional historians. These include climate apocalypse, the end of history, and species predestination for capitalism. The long-term stories of public consumption have often been at odds with each other, as with the climate story that declares that apocalypse is imminent without government intervention and the neo-liberal story that a free market

will automatically produce new forms of technology that will ameli-
orate the worst effects of climate change. History has the power of
destabilising such overarching stories. One of the most important
contributions of the Short Past was in the upsetting of mythologies of continental proportions, ones that had infected evolutionary
biology, economics, anthropology, and politics to their core. It is
possible to read the debates of economists debating policies for the
developing world from as recently as the 1960s, and to be astounded
at the invocation of race alongside historical traditions, by which we
learn that India and China had an innate lack of developmental
psychology in their abilities to relate to the material world and
therefore to all of technology and engineering. We no longer think
this way, largely because of the contributions of historians working in
the decades after 1975. The myth of white racial superiority, which
was revealed to have been forged with specious medical data. The
myth that the American Civil War was caused by a political doctrine
of states' rights rather than the abuses of slavery. The myth of the
benefits of western colonialism. The myth of western superiority.
The world would be a different place right now had those various
intellectual folklores not been excavated, cross-examined, and held
up to the light by a generation of critical historians who had taken
the cultural and postcolonial turns.

Historians no longer believe in the mythology that the world was
shaped dominantly for the good of economic well-being by the
influence of western empire, but many economists still do. Twenty
years ago, William A. Green explained how every rewriting of history
that changes when we think an event begins and ends offers an
opportunity for liberation from the 'intellectual straitjackets' that
define other fields.[51] One of the prime uses of data about the past is
to highlight instances of compulsive repetition, patterns that reveal
themselves in the archives. Long-term data about our past stand to
make an intervention in the confused debates of economists and
climate scientists merely by pointing out how experts become stuck
in old patterns of practice and ideology. Moreover, the digital data
now being mined by climate scientists and policy analysis – the data
of digitised newspapers, parliamentary records, and professional
journals – are data that reflect the work of modernity's institutions.
These archives likewise support a longer *durée* and a thicker contextual

reading than many dissertations manufactured in the last thirty years. But their *longue durée* is still the time-scale of decades or centuries.

An information society like ours needs synthesists and arbiters to talk about the use we make of climate data tables and economic indicators. It needs guides whose role is to examine the data being collected, the stories being told about it, and the actions taken from there, and to point out the continuities, discontinuities, lies, mismanagement, and outright confusion that occur in the process. But, above all, it needs to make those large stories comprehensible to the public it seeks to inform about future horizons and their meaning.

A sophisticated history that talks about where it gets its data has much to recommend it to a democratic society. In most of today's university disciplines, professional training serves to distance an individual from the public, to refine them into an 'expert' whose speech and writing are marked by incomprehensible formulae and keywords. But history-telling came out of an age before the era of experts, and its form is inherently democratic. Like story-telling or soccer, history is an activity that every man, woman, and child has access to, which they can pursue themselves, if only through keyword search, the local history archives, or the tracing of names on old gravestones.[52] Shaped into stories, that most ancient human tool for relating memory, history condenses enormous data about the past into a transmissible packet which expands into a rich brew of material for understanding things to come. Talking about the future in terms of our shared past is a method that opens up the possibility that anyone may submit an alternate position on where our future should go. They can always examine the evidence for themselves and disagree with the experts.

For example, if a complex, globalising world such as ours is to come to a position on climate change beyond the ejection of the poor to starvation or perpetual displacement and statelessness, it will need a democratic conversation about our past and possible avenues towards the future. Put to the service of the public future, history can cut through the fundamentalisms of scientists and economists who preach elite control of wealth or scientific monitoring of all earth systems as the only possible way to avoid catastrophe. History can open up other options, and involve the public in the dialogue and reimagination of many possible sustainabilities.

Popular long-term argumentation, whether about the climate, international government, or inequality, often takes the form of reasoning with many different kinds of events from long ago. A popular history like Jared Diamond's *Collapse: How Societies Choose to Fail or Succeed* (2005) weaves together a gripping account of the fates of societies stricken by plague, mixing archaeological evidence with the history of species extinction and ethnic deracination. Yet even such a book lacks the level of deep engagement that was characteristic of historians of the Short Past like Natalie Zemon Davis or Robert Darnton. In their intense reckoning with archives, historians had to grapple with many kinds of data – the fairytale, the archival artifact, the book itself and its binding and illustrations. To weave stories about obscure families and individuals who had never been written about before, micro-historians became masters of using multiple kinds of evidence – archaeological, architectural, statistical, technological, economic, political, and literary – to fill in the story of how the past was lived. Micro-history and other studies in the Short Past reached heights of sophistication in the constrained inspection of experience in the past; they were masters at using data of multiple kinds. What the Short Past still must teach us is the art of looking closely at all the details, when the longest-term perspective possible is not always the most relevant. A. J. P. Taylor once quipped that looking for long-term causes was like a car driver telling a police officer that he blamed his crash on the invention of the internal combustion engine.[53] When we overlook the details, questions about the big picture may slip away – no longer answered by data, but answered by speculation with the data used as marginalia.

There are few brighter examples of reductionism and its opposite than the debates over inequality in Victorian Britain, a subject that formed a major area of research for historians who grew up during the era of training in the Short Past. The Victorian period has been researched and written about in both History and Economics departments as a major concentration of the field. Yet the two fields could not disagree more about what happened. Each measures a single index or perhaps compares to indices of well-being: criminality and height; education and wealth at death; migration and wages. Based upon these data, some economists conclude that the nineteenth century led to gains in equality, opportunity, and entrepreneurship. Among economic historians dealing with inequality over the nineteenth century, a surprising number conclude that nineteenth-century industrialisation resulted in more nutrition for the poor, while twentieth-century 'socialism' resulted in higher taxes and stagnating social opportunity.[54] According to economists, these numbers demonstrate conclusively that capitalism banished inequality during the nineteenth century, and could do so again.

From the perspective of more radical historians, the Victorian experience was characterised by police suppression, the demonisation and abuse of the poor by new political institutions, and, ultimately, by extreme efforts towards class-consciousness and political organisation on behalf of the poor and racial minorities. Rich evidence about the growth of the state and the increase in welfare provision over a century tends to suggest other measures, and a more even-handed account, sometimes challenging the state as an authoritarian source of class divides, sometimes raising questions about whether civic power from below is channelled through print technology or face-to-face speech.[55] In dozens of books and articles published about the same locations and times as the economists have covered, historians have examined the diaries and pamphlets of mill workers to the accounts of food disbursed in prisons to lawsuits brought by the poor against workhouse administrators who starved or whipped them contrary to official regulations – a much denser set of evidence than the economists have looked at.[56] As a result of their different modalities of collecting data, historians' articles open up other suggestions for the future, including the importance of participatory democracy, but they very rarely confirm that the Industrial Revolution placed Victorian England on a model path towards civil accord, relative income equality, and opportunity for all.

Even the same events can be characterised in very different ways depending on how deeply layered the data are. For instance, the falling price of grain for workers during the 1870s has been celebrated by economists who model the history of growth in a 2002 paper as a demonstration that capitalism since 1500, despite deepening income inequality, ultimately created 'real purchasing power' for everyone, including the working class.[57] That same result of cheap food has a contrasting interpretation among historians as the product, to be sure, of decades of labour organising on behalf of

Manchester workers concerned about being unable to afford to eat. In fact, the moment of falling inequality around 1870 arguably had less to do with the rise of international trade, and more to do with the rise of organised labour after decades of state suppression, a moment made possible by working-class people insistently gathering in public to share their ideas and experience and organise a programme of political reform.[58] That is, of course, a story about social actors; hardly a victory to be credited to the account of free-market capitalism. Yet data are abused when they are examined as a single facet of historical experience. Both positive and negative assessments from the past from economics abstract single dimensions of experience—wages, the price of grain, or height—as a proxy for freedom, democracy or happiness.[59]

To take a more concrete example, there is the way that historians and economists both understand progress in the British Industrial Revolution. Decades earlier, American economists performed a study of the nutrition of poor people over the course of the nineteenth century, as documented in the height and weight of individuals when first admitted to prison. The evidence seemed to suggest that poor people were earning better wages – in general, earnings in 1867 had more purchasing power than had had in 1812.[60] But decades later, some British economists reconsidered the data, having spent some time reading up on British social history. The data confirmed, counter to the original thesis, that the weight of working-class women actually went down over the course of the Industrial Revolution. What we now understand is that the mothers and wives of working-class men had been starving themselves – skipping meals, passing on the bigger serving – to make sure that their mill-working or ship-loading husbands had enough energy to survive their industrial jobs. When first admitted to prison, most of the working-class women in English prisons were so thin and frail that they actually *gained* weight on the few cups of meagre gruel regulated by national authorities to deter lazy paupers from seeking welfare at houses of correction.[61]

The prison study reminds us, *pace* neo-liberal histories of the Industrial Revolution, of the way that class and gender privilege annihilated the victories of entrepreneurial innovation in the experience of the majority. Without a sensitivity to gender and age, the kind of sensitivity that the Cambridge economist Sara Horrell calls 'the wonderful usefulness of history' and attributes to her reading of historians of the Short Past, the evidence they looked at merely reinforced the prejudices of their field that Victorian industrialisation produced taller, better-fed proletarians.[62] Even in the field of big data, the sensitivity to agency, identity, and personhood associated with the Short Past has much to contribute to our epistemology and method.

The inequality debate is only one example of the way that, over some thirty years, certain economic historians have clung to conclusions about the economy forged decades or centuries before. Indeed, this trend has even been evident to other economists. Journals in the field have erupted into fits, as professors file back through articles over the decades that show how their colleagues have failed to consider conflicting models in their research, for the love of a particular hypothesis or mathematical display of rigour. In 2008, economist Karl Persson flew after his colleague Greg Clark for propounding what he called 'the Malthus delusion' against evidence that human civilisations usually contain their reproduction, and that poverty and want are therefore due to more complex factors than over-population alone. Persson accuses Clark of cherry-picking his data, looking at cross-sections and ignoring other economic historians who have already demolished the theory: 'When the historical record contradicts Greg Clark it is not allowed to stand in the way of his noble aim and declared intention of writing big history.' Persson continues: 'Clark does not surrender. Facts are not allowed to kill big history.'[63] When neo-liberal economists measure one factor over time not many, they are involved in speculation not long-term thinking.

For history to be usable by the present, it needs to be small enough that historians can do what they do best: comparing different kinds of data side by side. In traditional history, multiple causality is dealt with under the heading of different aspects of history – intellectual history, art history, or history of science – which reflect a reality forged by many hands. The reality of natural laws and the predominance of pattern do not bind individuals to any particular fate: within their grasp, there still remains an ability to choose. An historical outlook reminds the public that there are multiple causes at work for any event in the past – and as a result, that more than one favourable outcome is possible in the future.

CHAPTER 3

The long and the short
Climate change, governance, and inequality since the 1970s

Long-term thinking about the past and the future proliferates outside the discipline of history, notably around questions of climate change, international governance, and inequality. In all of these domains, the past is already being used as a tool with which to contemplate the future.

In discussions of climate, scientists have used the past to formulate warnings about how environmental destruction will affect our planetary future. In the decades after Rachel Carson's early warnings about the ecological consequences of pollution, the first terrifying pronouncements were published to the world forecasting planetary holocausts if changes were not made. In 1968, the American ecologist Garrett Hardin published his seminal article on the 'tragedy of the commons', comparing an over-populated planet to a wilderness preserve grazed excessively by wildlife. In announcing the limited carrying-capacity of the planet, and forecasting starvation and death for the many, Hardin's narrative paralleled the story of the expulsion from the Garden of Eden.[1] As biologists like Paul Ehrlich confirmed that extensive species extinction was a reality, they too articulated their fears about the future through the Malthusian vocabulary of testing, judgement, and despair.[2]

Through the 1970s, these claims about an imminent future were sharpened and refined in the course of data-driven analysis, political debate, and mounting impatience. In 1972, a newly founded global think-tank, the Club of Rome, issued a rousing report on environmental futures, funded by the Volkswagen Foundation, *Limits to Growth*, which publicised the new computer models of a systems analyst at the Massachusetts Institute of Technology, Jay Forrester, who warned against overshoot and collapse driven by over-population, pollution, and resource depletion. The book sold 12 million copies. At the same time, a report to the United Nations World Conference on the Human Environment endorsed the *Limits to Growth* report's conclusions of imminent doom, warning against both the reckless pursuit of economic success science and the nation-state itself.[3] At a variety of scales, scientific, governmental, and private organisations endorsed the view of impending ecological peril requiring immediate action.

Since the 1970s, pressure to rethink our relationship to the ecosystem has borne the mark of a quasi-apocalyptic form of long-term thinking, which moves from our sins in the industrial past directly to imminent destruction in the long-term future. Around the time of Rachel Carson's exposé, stories prognosticating doom arrived at almost exactly the moment of the last great recapitulation of popular apocalyptic religion in the United States, conceptualised in Hal Lindsay's best-selling story of the Rapture, *The Late Great Planet Earth* (1970), which became the largest-selling American non-fiction book of the 1970s.[4] Scientific predictions helped to kick off a new wave of apocalyptic speculation in American popular religion.

The apocalyptic diagnosis of our relationship to past and future continues to exert a pull on scientific discussions of climate change, shaping analysis even as the understanding of the climate is broadened and refined. In the early 2000s, a new narrative of collapse appeared which, following the work of entomologist E. O. Wilson on colony collapse, compared the history of civilisations to over-driven ecosystems, the most prominent of which compared industrial capitalism to the vanished civilisation of Easter Island and forecast the extinction of the human race. Piles of scientific evidence have been amassed since the 1970s, but our long-term thinking has shifted little if at all from the terrors of that moment. We still reason largely in terms of apocalypse, as if we are afraid that without final judgement on our future we will be unable to summon the collective courage to shift from an unsustainable future to a sustainable one as we live in what is alleged to be our 'final century', even 'our final hour'.[5]

It is not our purpose here to question the accumulation of evidence about the past that scientists have amassed since the 1970s, but rather to call attention to certain patterns in the historical interpretation of those results. Since the 1950s, climate science has expanded and refined into a new profession, which has established certainty about global climate shocks and proved that beyond mere pollution and resource exhaustion, the planet is now facing both global warming and rising sea-levels.[6] The problem is not that the climate science community does not have data about these events: it has immense amounts of it, regarding many historical events and trends. What is important here is that the overarching narrative wrapped around those events has largely remained one of apocalypse. In scientific discourse, more data should result in new conclusions. In historical accounts, likewise: more data should result in refined and expanded metanarratives.[7]

Indeed, critiques of scientists' sense of time have been voiced from the discipline of economics. In the wake of the 2006 British government-sponsored Stern Review on the Economics of Climate Change, apocalyptic warnings and cries for immediate action led to a denunciation by economists who clamoured against 'the assumption of a near-zero time discount rate' in scientists' modelling of possible futures. In other words, the narrative of certain doom had left too little room for future contingencies in which entrepreneurs suddenly came up with more energy-intensive technologies that produced far fewer emissions than the ones in use today.[8] Even left-leaning economists calculated that at least fifty more years of unimpeded growth lay ahead (some said far more), and that it would be immoral to deprive the developing nations of their possible economic future on the basis of a theory. Economists' models of future temporality were in conflict with climatologists'.

To counter the claims of climate scientists about rising CO_2 and a changing climate that merited immediate action, some economists proposed their own version of past and future, one that emphasised continuous technological innovation and economic growth since 1700. Others proposed that no matter what dangers had recently been revealed by climate science, the invisible hand of the market would take care of them all.[9] Neither side really substantiated their claims by taking into account the others. Instead, both sides had mutually irreconcilable models of the past based on limited data of their own.

The problem with these stories is not that they are wrong *per se*, but rather that they are reductionist; mere cartoon-versions of long-term thinking about the past without the scale and nuance that might yet be possible. Wherever we see the persistence of reductionist stories about time – whether apocalyptic stories propounded by environmental scientists like Jared Diamond or cornucopian stories composed by economists like Nobel laureate Douglass North – we read evidence that scientists have not consulted their own data when narrating their history. Nor is it really their job to forge this kind of interpretation – of actors, events, responsibilities, and solutions. We need long-term data on the climate and economy to tell us when someone notices that the earth is changing. The second level of analysis – assigning responsibility, finding concomitant recommendations about how the earth should be reformed to prevent greater catastrophe still – requires skills of working back and forth between past and future, discerning multiple sources of causality and ranking them, examining them from different perspectives and experiences to offer the fullest possible account of how the catastrophe came to be and therefore what is owed to whom. That kind of thinking about the past, compiling cases for possible vectors of reform, has always been the purview of neither science nor economics but of history.

LONG-TERM THINKING ABOUT THE CLIMATE

But no one can blame those worried about the environment for trying. What climate science has grasped since 1970, in its insistence on reasoning about past and future, is the absolute necessity of making claims about causality if we are indeed to change our behaviour from forms of economic behaviour known to jeopardise both humans and other living organisms. Thinking with history has always been a tool for reshaping the future, whether that intervention takes the form of time on the therapist's couch remembering one's childhood, the collective examination of national or planetary sins in the past, re-running scenarios of historical decision-making, or forming policy through the carefully contextual handling of evidence.[10]

For all of those reasons, when scientists have sought to establish human culpability in climate change and call for future action, they have found themselves in the realm of historical reasoning. In the midst of policy wars between economists and climate scientists, history has become a trump card played by both sides in order to

secure their argument about the nature of our world and the necessary conditions of a sustainable future. Indeed, one might say that a
great deal of climate science now concerns less the extension of new
models of ecosystem or biology, and more the reckoning of historical
problems. Scientists now spend a great deal of their energy establishing agreed-upon timelines for the human cause of climate change, a
conversation never far away from calls for a change in national and
international policy towards the environment. The 'Anthropocene'
was first proposed as a concept in 2000 by Nobel laureate Paul
Crutzen, an atmospheric chemist, who identified the era as a new
epoch in terms of planetary geology, comparable to the Holocene or
Paleocene in its difference from previous epochs.[11] As Australian
historian Libby Robin records, Crutzen's intervention 'was a bold
statement on many levels', not least because it was the first geological
epoch ever proposed that included the future – the accumulated
effects of anthropogenic activity – as well as the past.[12] The label
immediately resulted in a historical debate over whether the effects of
climate change began 250 years ago with the steam engine, eleven
thousand years ago with the rise of human hunter civilisations and
the extinction of animals, or five to eight thousand years ago with the
agricultural revolution.[13] At issue were not so much the numbers, as
how scientists assigned causality to past events. Was the domesti-
cation of the cow and rice to blame for later patterns of cutting down
rainforests that would not appear for millennia to come? In a sudden
turn of events, the major public battle engaged in by climate scientists was in essence a controversy about history.

Thinking with the past still offers most of the solutions that have
been proposed in debates about climate change. A number of scientists today stress the need for 'earth systems governance', or 'carbon
trading', looking to the evidence of human history to provide models
of government or market capable of remedying disasters like this
one.[14] In so doing, they typically seek to replicate other state infrastructure projects, where nations have assumed responsibility for
preserving life into the future, from the government-built dykes of
the early-modern Netherlands to the American Manhattan Project in
the Second World War and on to the World Bank-organised credit
programmes from a decade ago inspired by the writings of Hernando
de Soto.[15] Nor must all the possible historical precedents for coherent

environmental change necessarily take the shape of centralised authority. Indeed, climate scientists have begun to construct models of climate change that focus on the specific ways in which tribes of humans have shaped the biosphere, foregrounding sustainable and unsustainable patterns of land use as models for the future.[16] Questions about which options to choose and how have driven a new generation of scientists trained as biologists, chemists, and geologists to become, effectively, historians of institutions.

That same impetus has begun to transform the discipline of economics as well. Economists like Anil Markandya have used historical thinking to cut the Gordian knot of growth vs ecology. Markandya revisited questions of environmental regulation with new data gathered over a century and a half from the experience of regulation in Britain. His conclusion was that Britain had started regulating sulphur dioxide and other contaminants as early as 1821, all 'without any serious impact on GDP per capita'.[17] Historical data like Markandya's prove that it is possible to refute doctrine about the trade-offs between innovation and ecology.[18] In this way, history proves capable of expanding our sense of options for the future, and discerning which theories of the future are appropriate given the historical and present data that we have on hand. The successes of enormous collective investment strategies in the past provide the justification for a radical rethinking of climate governance for the future.

Historically minded scientists and economists have been joined by ecologically minded historians. Under pressure of stories about the Anthropocene, long-term histories of land and water use have become increasingly precise in their accounts of where ecological stress has happened before, why, and how it has been overcome. Some of that work confirms that the West has been on a long path to environmental exhaustion, moving from one energy source to another, generation by generation, a process that helped to give rise to the modern nation-state, at the time a form of 'international government' of unprecedented size and strength. That was the answer that historian Paul Warde has now provided to a starting question of striking relevance – how was it that early-modern Europe had survived an ecological crisis of unprecedented scale? – that required him to invent a new way of doing history, essentially one that required modelling big data over three centuries of information in obscure archives. Over the course of years, travelling from small town to small town, Warde began adding up all of the illegal infractions that happen over centuries, relating them to climate events, and judging how our ancestors found a way out. In this account, new forms of governance become important in reaction to environmental exhaustion, at times when fighting over a collapsing ecosystem results in anarchy that only a new form of government can resolve.[19]

A similar pattern of looking to the long past for alternative solutions for the future has been pursued in the domain of water by the prolific Norwegian historian and geographer Terje Tvedt, past president of the International History of Water Association, who has presided over a six-volume history of water from the administration of irrigation in ancient China to water-wars in contemporary Africa.[20] For Tvedt, questions of survival meant developing an almost encyclopaedic knowledge of water as resource and scourge in the history of civilisation, learning how it had shaped governments, military strategy, farming, governance, and engineering projects over not centuries but millennia. Surveying examples of solutions and crises from melting glaciers and rising sea-levels to desertification and water-wars, Tvedt stresses the immense vulnerability of our present-day economies to rising sea-levels. A world history of the past becomes for him a reservoir of possible contingencies and alternative futures, each of which will be pitted against the other, overturning the old geography of immovable centres of finance and manufacturing in coastal cities like Shenzhen, London, and New York in favour of water-rich regions like Greenland and Tibet.[21]

Other historians, bent by similar questions of survival and crisis over the long term, have been driven to big data that shows how historical cities may offer new models for sustainable economies to come, proving that not all western history confirms the rule of resource exhaustion. French historians Sabine Barles and Gilles Billen have measured nineteenth-century Paris in terms of its human waste, river pollution, and nitrogen impact, collecting data from government sanitary authorities and the city toll-gates. Why toll-gates? Because for much of the medieval era into the nineteenth century, city officials stopped and taxed wagons from the countryside on their way to city markets. They left behind a complete list of how much food the city of Paris consumed. Together with government records from the 1860s, when Paris began to invest in modern sewerage treatment, we have a complete record of Paris' 'nitrogen footprint', stretching back over hundreds of years.[22] It allows us to tell a richer story of the way in which our near ancestors lived in relationship with their land.

Data mined over generations in the past can give us insight into the future of sustainability. Barles conjectures that nineteenth-century Paris can offer more in terms of a capitalist city that nonetheless was more sustainable, in terms of local agriculture and waste recycling, than the twenty-first-century cities of today. Barles has published some of her historical research with an audience of policy-makers in development in mind. Indeed, Barles is only one of the historians who delved back into urban records to find the story of how nineteenth-century managers invented sustainable practices for waste reuse in large cities.[23] Could the nineteenth century offer a paradigm of a city worth returning to, a city still brimming with entertainment and consumption and global trade, but which nonetheless depended on nearby farms for its produce? History can open up new possibilities, expanding the array of policy and market futures available past carbon trading and earth systems governance into a wider array of possible sustainabilities.

Examples of events from the deep or recent past alike can point to alternative traditions in governance, collecting and describing the fringe movements of the past that are bearing useful fruit today. Joan Thirsk ploughed five centuries of the past for examples of moments similar to the present, when shifting dynamics around land and water caused a search for a more sustainable agriculture. Paul B. Thompson has given a remarkable overview of the historical sources for conservation, organic farming, and sustainable building. Martin Mulligan and Stuart Hill have written a history of permaculture.[24] Histories such as these perform an important role: they are energising of new movements; they give scientists and policy-makers on the ground a sense of where to look for possible futures.

That opening up of possibilities and alternative models has revolutionary potential in a world where most models of the future cluster around climate change-induced doom or invisible hand-managed versions of the status quo. Suddenly, it looks like historical civilisations and recent environmental activists can offer models of sustainability that can feed the poor and house the refugees of rising sea-levels, if only there is political will. Such a message of hope, and such a recipe for focused action, can act as a salve for minds troubled by spectacles of apocalypse or mantras of rational choice. It is medicine for reasoned action in our time, using knowledge of the past, rather than fantasy or dogma, as a tool with which to shape the future. As Libby Robin writes:

The future is no longer destined. Rather, it is something we 'create'. . . . If so, we need to engage all possible creativity in making that future: science, economics, history and the human imagination. No one can predict the future, but imagination can illuminate its relationship to history and the present condition of the world.[25]

Written at the nexus of past and future, history can draw a map that includes not only pictures of the fantasy world of capitalistic success and the world burning in climate change apocalypse, but also realistic alternative pathways to a world that we actually *want* to inhabit. These stories can open up new ways of thinking and escape old nightmares: 'The Anthropocene … is not a parable of human hubris, but rather a call to realize our fullest potential as managers of the earth and our future on it.'[26]

In order to repair the work of broken models of the long term, the work of thinking with time will have to take on not only these positive future potentialities, but also the reality of the obstacles that have historically stood in our way to accomplishing a more just, sustainable, or ecologically attuned civilisation. Here, too, historians have already been at work. History can also point the finger, directing blame towards those responsible for harm or who have slowed down more revolutionary processes with less revolutionary means. Joshua Yates has offered a preliminary decades-long history of ideas of sustainability, sketching for us how the terms of the debate have been constructed at institutions such as the Columbia Business School, which churns out an array of 'chief sustainability officers' who promise to protect people, the planet, and prosperity, but only through altering patterns of consumption among the world's elite.[27] The marshalling of scarce resources to stymie the worst effects of climate change on behalf of an elite, no matter the consequences for the rest of the population, has a history. There are institutions, individuals, and educational programmes that shaped greenwashing, and reviewing their past can help us to choose other institutions for the future – for instance the state agriculture extension programme in Australia, which has converted its materials for small farmers from ones that focus on petro-chemical fertilisers and pesticides to ones that emphasise the emerging science of permaculture.[28]

With longer perspectives, the directives that history gives can be much clearer still. Swedish historians Andreas Malm and Alf Hornborg have observed that the key event in Paul Crutzen's account of climate change is the invention and proliferation of the steam engine. Looked at in terms of the history of empires and capitalism, the trajectory towards intensifying pollution, agriculture, and consumption from the steam engine forward is not shared equally by all members of the species. Reviewing decades of micro-historical work on the nature of capitalism and empire, Malm and Hornborg are able to point the finger at a particular, small subset of western elite families and corporations, who they believe share the blame for the climate disruption. As Malm and Hornborg write, 'The rationale for investing in steam technology at this time was geared to the opportunities provided by the constellation of a largely depopulated New World, Afro-American slavery, the exploitation of British labour in factories and mines, and the global demand for inexpensive cotton cloth'. The species as a whole can hardly be equally to blame for climate change, or equally responsible for cleaning it up. They explain, 'A significant chunk of humanity is not party to the fossil economy at all: hundreds of millions rely on charcoal, firewood or organic waste such as dung for all domestic purposes'.[29]

Histories of how ruling powers in the West employed expert civil engineers, foresters, and agronomists to discount unilaterally the wisdom of local peoples managing their land have stressed the way that capitalism, the nation-state, and rule by landlords are directly related to the environmental destruction that characterises the last two hundred years of the Anthropocene. Evidence of the rise of the doctrine of 'improvement' in Enlightenment Europe gives us a hint of the way new ideas about class and racial superiority, not merely economic strategising, tipped the sudden accumulation of power into the hands of a few landlords at the dawn of the industrial age, leading to a new ideology that wedded power to the exploitation of the environment.[30]

Given this accumulation of historical evidence, it is no longer tenable to hold the view that links our current environmental predicament with so remote a cause as the evolutionary inheritance of humankind as an inherently greedy and destructive species. As Malm and Hornborg write:

Capitalists in a small corner of the Western world invested in steam, laying the foundation stone for the fossil economy: at no moment did the species vote for it either with feet or ballots, or march in mechanical unison. To invoke ultra-remote causes of this kind 'is like explaining the success of the Japanese fighter pilots in terms of the fact that prehumans evolved binocular vision and opposable thumbs. We expect the causes we cite to connect rather more directly to consequences', or else we disregard them ... Attempts to attribute climate change to the nature of the human species appear doomed to this sort of vacuity. Put differently, transhistorical – particularly species-wide – drivers cannot be invoked to explain a qualitatively novel order in history, such as mechanized, steam-power production of commodities for export to the world-market.[31]

If Malm and Hornborg are correct, the human history of climate change points us in a different direction – towards the responsibility of the developed world and the corporations that have contributed the most to and benefited the most from climate change.

In cases such as these, history offers us instruction about the arrangement of political economy itself, controverting the accepted wisdom that the regulation of industries and taxation of vested interests hampers economic growth. It upsets the policy stalemate of the 1990s, one that could be characterised as environmentalists preaching more regulation and international cooperation, with economists preaching self-interest, technological innovation, and deregulation and promising that environmental solutions would only come further down the road. Largely because of the evidence about long-term processes amassed by historians, that stalemate is no longer tenable. Historical evidence in economics has already substantiated the fact that economic growth is still possible in such a regulatory climate. Historical reasoning here also lays a path towards governance systems that penalise the interests that have benefited the most from climate destruction.

As we begin probing historical data for issues of causality, agency, and alternatives, we learn that the 'tragedy of the commons' is not a necessary rule, but rather a historically constructed set of conditions about destroying the commons set up by western elites for their own ends.[32] We learn that the terms 'carrying capacity' and even 'over-population' or 'population' carry with them the imprint of colonial ideas about wildlife management and management of natives and indigenous people, or even of religious ideas about God's punishment intended for the lazy, and that they have been less substantiated as an actual law of nature than was once supposed.[33] In reviewing outmoded ideas and demonstrating the burden of ancient prejudice over fact, history can offer a critical rethinking of the terms we use to talk about the future, demonstrating how certain kinds are stamped with prejudice or outmoded thinking.

The genre of history illustrated by Robin, Yates, and Thompson is history at its most critical. They identify the players who are constructing the game; they show where the terms came from, and they point out contradictions in the system. Critical history is one of the forms of story-telling that most historians today are trained to perform. Critical history can help us to tell which logics to keep for the future and which to throw away. Stamped with the 'hermeneutics of suspicion', critical history is the child of the 1970s just as much as micro-history is, although it has a rich legacy going back at least to Karl Marx. It is fruitfully applied to the purpose of unmasking institutional corruption – finding toxic discourses with laden or implicit meanings; unveiling supposed saviours as frauds; disrobing would-be emperors. We have a lot of good critical history. Nathan Sayre tells us how the term 'carrying capacity' was first applied to boats, which would literally sink if their capacity were over-reached; it was then transferred to animal populations in the case of British colonial monitoring of hunting reserves, and later passed from the colonial government of animals to the governance of native populations.[34] Implicit in the term are the logics of top-down government control of population. Similar findings have been suggested by Alison Bashford's and Matthew Connelly's histories of international government, population control, and neo-Malthusianism.[35] Of all of the kinds of control we can put into place, history suggests, the control of population is one of the most likely to go awry.

The implications for international policy of all of this sorting into fact and fiction are immense. Indeed, this form of historical reasoning directly controverts the international policy embraced by most nations since the Brundtland Commission in 1987, which reasoned that developed nations could not shoulder the burden of ameliorating climate change, because of their relationship to ongoing industrialisation projects in the Global South.[36] In this example, species thinking – insisting that we as a species must cooperate together – has served as a convenient excuse for western elites to deny that they are in a position to respond to a changing climate. Historical reasoning, including the postcolonial history embraced by elites in India and China, gives western powers no such veil of economic theory as an excuse for doing nothing.

THINKING ABOUT INTERNATIONAL GOVERNANCE

The power of historical thinking to destabilise conclusions about the best shape of institutions extends beyond questions of the environment. In matters of international governance, thinking about the past also marks almost all conversations. If we look backwards over the last fifty years, to many historians it appears that socialism is dead in the water, killed by what historian Angus Burgin has called 'the great persuasion', the organised assertion of free-market principles by European and American think-tanks founded by libertarian economists but shaped and promoted, often against the better judgements of those economists themselves, into an advocacy lobby for the interests of large-scale American corporations.[37] In the battles between institutions that followed in the 1970s and 1980s, a new era of 'globalisation' or 'neo-liberalism' emerged, characterised by the vanishing of socialism and trade unions, the collapse of communism as an alternative, the rise of international institutions like the International Monetary Fund (IMF), WTO, World Bank, G-7, G-8, and other supranational gatherings intended to extend credit, trade, and entrepreneurship worldwide.[38] In this model, the global corporation, technology, and national government go hand in hand; they form a natural bulwark that stands beyond question as the only conceivable cure for any society's ills. In this vein, the CEO of Google and the director of its think-tank, Google Ideas, for instance, argued for high technology as the ally of democratic national policy, ending poverty and opening up the media and elections.[39] The leaders who propose solutions for the future are not reformers or activists but entrepreneurs and CEOs.

Until recently, it was rare for a journalist or policy-maker to handle these institutions as products of history about which it was possible to raise questions. These transitions have to be understood as historical watersheds, and what they mean and whether they have worked is matter for critical thinking about long-term change. Much of the conversation about these institutions has instead come from individuals who were major players in policy themselves. Their testimony unequivocally celebrates the emergence of new institutions by declaring a new historical era, rather than asking what that era has done. From the United States, at least, it looks like 'socialism is dead'. For Samuel Huntington, the long-term struggles of Europe against the rest of the world signalled the perpetuation of these conflicts into the future. For Francis Fukuyama, the downfall of the Soviet Union marked 'the end of history', or a moment when no other utopian projects than capitalism were for the moment imaginable.[40] Are any of those claims about the past really true? How would we know?

Such claims as these have lately been subjected to big-data testing in the hands of political scientists assembling new datasets on world cultures and institutions over the *longue durée*, who hope to use these datasets to test theories about whether cultural conflict is inevitable. Since Huntington predicted a 'clash of civilisations' in the 1990s, scholars in political science and International Relations have been formulating statistical databases to measure the regularity and nature of inter-state disputes. These analyses have shown little consensus about the nature of conflict or the trajectory of history, even when they agree that economic aid and growth overall tend to have a positive correlation with democracy.[41] Indeed, many have questioned the viability of Huntington's category of 'civilisations', itself a concept borrowed from the essentialising, hierarchical worldview of Victorian anthropology, and questionably applicable to a globalised world characterised by cross-national education, trade, and migration.[42] Even with immense data-gathering, then, the formulae for understanding our past and future that were most influential in the 1990s and 2000s turn out to be less than persuasive. Where else then can we look for guidance?

An alternative is to look to the power of history to name alternative systems of governance. One instance is the *longue-durée* story offered by David Graeber in his *Debt: The First 5,000 Years* (2010). While scholars of international studies in the wake of Margaret Thatcher have maintained that indeed there is no alternative to capitalism, Graeber shows how capitalist concepts of debt are only the most recent instance of a recurring form of culture that holds debt against individuals, and that cumulatively the historical record of debt-systems is a generations-long, cross-continental chain of slavery by which strangers are bound to strangers before the time of their birth. With this history, Graeber is able to hold up the real historical alternatives with which Buddhist monasteries and prophetic Christian sects answered debt chains when they found them, alternatives based upon the abolition of debt at regular intervals. Graeber recommends such remission both for the international debts that bind developing nations to the World Bank and to the internal debts that increasingly shackle college graduates and working-class consumers in the United States. Graeber's story depends upon interweaving thousands of analyses of different economics systems ranging from aboriginal Madagascar to the Kwakiutl Indians to the African experience of the transatlantic slave trade in the era just before the American Civil War. None of these episodes is a static system; instead, all of them are coming up against each other, running into trans-oceanic trade networks, and being challenged or challenging back as a result. With this picture, Graeber is able to show that various forms of money relationships, from the gift to the debt, have been around for a long time, and that they do not sit easily with each other, and that the indebted and enslaved have recourses at their disposal, including prophecy and revolution. A series of micro-episodes leads up to a macro-vision of the world which is critically larger than the one we had before.[43]

Stories like Graeber's stand to destabilise our faith in structures like debt itself as most conducive to a kind of democracy characterised by participation and opportunity. While Huntington and Fukuyama were engaged in shaping history into a simple allegory about the triumph of the West, the long-term perspective opens up doors and windows, allowing us to look around at other ways of organising our society. A longer history of international government can even demonstrate that alternatives exist to our own political system, alternatives that might in turn offer a fuller expression of the concept of democracy itself. New data-driven surveys raise questions about inevitability of the 'Westphalian' state, the only form of governance that has been truly universalised since the late eighteenth century. In this model, every human must be – or aspires to be – a member of such a state; almost every inch of the earth's surface is claimed and controlled by these states.[44] But is this model truly the one that has staying power and utopian potential in the twenty-first century?

Before the present moment, a series of emerging attempts at world governments have taken noticeably different tacks. The League of Nations sought to create a lasting peace by unifying the voices of democratic government. As Mark Mazower has shown, in the 1940s leaders combined a faith in the virtue of national planning with a commitment to participation in collective international decision-making bodies. The United Nations expanded this vision, wedding to it a vision of expertise deployed to the advantage of the developing world, with cooperative experts sent by the International Labor Organization (ILO) and soil experts sent by the Food and Agriculture Organization (FAO), with housing and educational specialists extending knowledge around the globe. The World Bank was originally organised to support these visions of world government in lifting up the economic power of the developing world but by the 1970s, it had taken a new line of experimentation – the extension of gigantic national debts – ostensibly intended to help the nations of Latin America, Africa, and South Asia to build their infrastructure. In fact, the rise of the World Bank signalled a transition to a new form of international government, one where international finance, not a growing tax base, were supposed to supply needed revenue for large-scale projects.[45] Around 1970, the record suggests, the promise of international government in support of democracy was broken. The forms of international government we have had ever since have favoured large corporations and entrenched interests rather than development or democracy.

Does international government have any sort of a future today? Increasingly, Brazil, Russia, India, and China (the BRICs), the emerging countries, are getting cut out of deals. We have seen global movements and mass protests – the Arab Spring, the Occupy Movement, but also the Indignados in Spain; civil unrest in Istanbul, Kiev, and London; and looking back even further, the Millennium Development Goals (MDGs), the Human Rights movement, the growth of NGOs, Altermondialism, or peasant movements like the Via Campesina. Could these movements point to a new direction in global governance? This question, too, is being addressed through serious work with historical fact. Historians have documented the rise of an international indigenous peoples' movement since the 1970s, drawing attention to the reality of institutions often ignored by media or political science. They have demonstrated the success of the Movimiento Sin Terra (the Landless People's Movement or MST), the landless people's movement of Brazil, and its programme of democratically administered peoples' agricultural movements.[46]

As to enterprise and technology, there are longer stories there, too, which can help us to imagine what a free market or economic growth might look like in a context in which democracy mattered. In the eighteenth century, nations started treating new technologies like road and rail as common resources, subsidising their development through eminent domain (also known as 'forced purchase', the doctrine of the state seizure of land for the public good) and forcing them to serve the poor through decreased tariffs and mandates to reach the poorer hinterlands. Since then, major powers have gone through many phases of government building and libertarian retrenchment.[47] Longer stories have begun to open up questions about the relationship between technology, the free market, and economic growth.

The technologies of global democracy, from the census to the Internet, suggest other ways in which technologies can be harnessed by the state. In our own time, there are other technologies that offer to extend the promise of political and market participation. These include participatory mapping of ecological disasters as pursued by 'citizen science' groups, dialogue, and democratic processes, the extension of cheap and free broadband to countrysides and ghettos, the enforcement of net neutrality to encourage entrepreneurship at all levels of capitalisation, and the democratisation of the Internet domain system out of the hands of the privately run Internet Corporation for Assigned Names and Numbers (ICANN). Initial histories of these movements suggest the way that innovation, even the invention of the Internet itself, can be tied to a history of state investment and broad-based political participation, often by those who have no links to power already.[48] But historians have started to understand that this search for a technology suited to participatory democracy has a much longer story, stretching back to the first decades of the twentieth century, when organisations like Mass Observation attempted to crowd-source data on unemployment and citizen-social scientists launched an intelligence campaign to protect Great Britain from fascism.[49]

As more stories have been gathered about these 'paths not taken', so too have historians gathered information about the pattern of expert rule that excludes democratic participation from the avenues of power. For example, in studies of the British administration of irrigation in India, the British administration of the *Anopheles* mosquito in Egypt, and the history of public health, historians have found ample evidence that many nation-states suppressed democracy from within, using expertise as a way to exclude citizen lobbies on the basis of race and class.[50] They have also shown that the growth of NGOs corresponds with the increasing side-lining of trade unions, neighbourhood groups, and even political parties from political process – with the result that the real financial power for new projects, whether poverty relief or education or environmental reform – is rarely held by voters.[51] Historical evidence even suggests that the proliferation of economists in high-profile policy positions has been linked to the promotion of GDP and the concomitant discounting of employment, health, education, and political participation.[52]

As with the debate on climate change, historical data can provide not only models worthy of emulation but also warnings, in this case about the dangerous effects of technology monopolies on national markets. Historical studies of American railroads show how government backing of unregulated private companies led to over-extension of resources in a world where no capital large enough to follow those interests existed. As a result, railway tycoons benefited, while millions of individual families lost the fortunes that they had invested in boomtowns that were economically speaking doomed from the start.[53] Other stories of state monopoly power have recently drawn the connection between corporate power and America's bloody history of extending a police state through Latin America, the Philippines, and Vietnam.[54]

INEQUALITY

Nowhere are determinations about blame and alternatives so heated as in conversations like these, which stress the distance between the haves and have-nots. Unsubstantiated myths about the *longue durée* persist, affirming that the institutions we have now are the only ones that we ever can have. The most powerful of these myths in our time are those about inequality. They have two major varieties: one, based in economic anthropology, which looks backwards to the existence of alpha male behaviour among primates, and insists that inequality is a known facet of our species behaviour, and therefore will never go away.[55] The other grand story about inequality and time is that associated with Cold War economist Simon Kuznets, a Harvard professor and former employee of the US War Department, whose data on the rise of living standards of most Americans between the Great Depression and the 1960s suggested that in a capitalist democracy inequality will naturally go away.[56] Over the thirty years after 1970, a time when history and the humanities were on the retreat from the public realm, stories like these circulated unchallenged in many fields of policy and academia. But today the return of long-term thinking is forcing scholars to question both myths with the power of factual data gathered over time.

The power of this data to transform argument has been graphically illustrated by the debates about long-term economic inequality under capitalism awakened by the publication of economist Thomas Piketty's *Capital in the Twenty-First Century* (2014).[57] Piketty explains in his introduction that his prompt for gathering *longue-durée* data about inequality was when he was told a statement that most economists accept as law: Kuznets' assertion that capitalism would, over time, tend to reduce inequality.[58] Kuznets based his principle on a few decades of data, not centuries, as Piketty would later, and this data came from an exceptional period in economic history – the period of post-depression and postwar recovery in which Kuznets himself was living, an era which was actually one of the most impressive periods of rising growth and falling inequality in the last two centuries.[59] But as Piketty examined the fortunes of inequality in France, America, Britain, and elsewhere over two hundred years, his evidence showed that falling inequality was actually quite unusual under capitalism. His *longue-durée* analysis shook the prejudices and supposed laws of economists, unveiling with the power of data what was supposedly conclusive truth as contingent speculation.

Piketty's intervention depended upon measuring many kinds of data against each other. The data on inequality were gathered from five different nations – France, Britain, America, Germany, and Sweden. It often forcibly approximated years for which no data were collected, and adjusted them to take into account the different national practices of doing accounts, or extrapolated them back across decades when census practices changed. As became clear when the *Financial Times* questioned Piketty's analyses, this juggling of data required asking critical questions about the nature of government numbers in the first place. Why, the *Financial Times* wanted to know, did Piketty claim that 70 per cent of Britain's contemporary wealth was in the hands of the 1 per cent, when government figures themselves said that only 35 per cent was held by the elite? As Piketty's public rebuttals and explanations made clear, he had already thought about these questions in great depth, and explained them in a series of articles. Government figures on wealth in Britain were self-reported, and they did not therefore encompass wealth hidden offshore.[60]

This kind of critical analysis of data has a long tradition in History departments, going back to Theodore Porter's and Ian Hacking's work in the 1970s, which showed how common government statistical definitions, from 'unemployment' to the 'average man', were calculated with a view of establishing political peace by minimising the case of the working class for reparations, welfare, or even government reform.[61] But a critical long-term analysis of data can call those averages and tabulations into question, helping to overturn old prejudices about the necessary state of politics or diffusion of wealth in a society. This is exactly the kind of intervention into world debates that Braudel hoped his *longue-durée* studies would lend themselves to.

Part of the power of Piketty's book was that his critique of Kuznets rested on data-driven methods for debunking historical myths propounded in economics on the basis of short-run data. Since the 1970s, economics has been stuck in an enduring debate over the results of more technology and productivity in society: does more innovation lead to greater wealth or leisure for all? Or does more technological innovation trap modern humans in a spiralling quest for consumable goods that take ever more time and effort, even as expanding cities require the working class to own an automobile to get to work in the first place?[62] Piketty's own interventions are also only a small part of a many-collaborator coalition to measure accurately the promises and reality of income inequality under advanced capitalism. Under the leadership of Piketty and Emmanuel Saez, the Paris School of Economics has made public a *longue-durée* database of top individual incomes around the world, aggregating data from public tax rolls, nation by nation, since 1900.[63]

Piketty's book – by his own admission, 'as much a work of history as of economics' – exemplifies the power of relevant historical studies, driven by data, to speak to policy and publics well beyond professional history.[64] History has this power to create major theoretical debates, revealing that what was previously accepted as a natural truth is actually no more than unexamined bias. As a result, *Capital in the Twenty-first Century* has disrupted the core beliefs of many of those who govern our society – especially those responsible for the Wall Street bailouts of 2010. At the core of the new controversy his history has inspired are claims about the nature and promise of capitalism itself, seen in the *longue durée* and conducted as a battle in which long-run analysis triumphs over short-run data.

THE PROLIFERATION OF MYTHOLOGY

The abundance of false stories in our time is one of the major reasons that we are in a crisis of short-term thinking. In an era of simplistic solutions to problems with rising sea-levels, governance, or inequality, few people can talk authoritatively about the big picture. The proliferation of reductionist stories about the past has a history, like anything else. Nightmare scenarios and fundamentalist mythologies about climate, governance, and inequality began to proliferate around the same time that historians began to retreat to shorter and shorter time scales.

As the Short Past came to dictate conversations about history, *longue-durée* understanding began to look, by contrast, like an antique mode of story-telling, something performed only by patriarchs or amateurs, unsuited to a modern student adept at using evidence or argument. This led to the charge that social history had abandoned all interest in politics, power, and ideology, leading its practitioners instead to 'sit somewhere in the stratosphere, unrooted in reality'.[65] Increasingly, the Short Past was defined as not only one way to look at history, but the *only* way to look at history.

By the end of the 1970s, the tendency to go long began to look tarnished, something grubby that no self-respecting historian would do. Furthermore, those historians still left in the *longue-durée* game were subject to pressures to report to readers divided by the impossibly conflicting opinions typical of the international scene during the Cold War. Consider the experience of Caroline Ware, editor of the *History of Mankind*, a multi-volume project commissioned by UNESCO and developed between 1954 and 1966. Ware's volume, submitted to civil servant reviewers of the nations represented by UNESCO, was subjected to an ideological tug-of-war between Russian and French readers, Protestant and Catholic reviewers, all of whom lobbied UNESCO for revisions that would reflect their own national and ideological understandings of world history. For someone working on behalf of an organ of international governance such as Ware, the success of the project depended upon making a synthesis that both communists and capitalists could agree with, and that task proved simply insurmountable. The lobbying for content was such that the project's staff were driven to near desperation about ever writing a synthetic history capable of working within the frame. Ware herself wrote in a letter that 'it is not possible to write a history of the 20th century'.[66] Such dispiriting experiences of writing for the organs of international government tarnished the genre of *longue-durée* history still further. Ware's frustration with rhetorical appeasement was something their micro-historian colleagues in the archives could avoid entirely. These experiences, and many others like them, provided a major rationale for a generation of historians to retreat from long-range history in general.

By and large, after this episode, historians as a cohort declined to engage with futurists, leaving 'dirty' *longue-durée* history in contra-distinction to micro-history as the tool of journalists and pundits, hardly a science at all, rarely assigned in the classroom, and almost never debated or emulated. Works of micro-history have expanded our understanding of peasant lives, the variety of psychological impulses, public and private, and the constructedness of human experience. But they have also largely abandoned the rhetorical practice, in their writing of history, of a larger moral critique available to non-historians as a source for alternative social formations over the *longue durée*.

In an era of ideological divisiveness, social scientists became increasingly sceptical that the institutions of international develop-ment could be ideologically neutral or effective as the promises of modernisation theory withered and died across the globe from Latin America and Southeast Asia, especially after the Vietnam War.[67] Their bibliographies, in contrast with those of the previous gener-ation, would accordingly be increasingly filled with publications in peer-reviewed journals not with contributions to the ballooning grey literature of international organs. Their retreat was wholesale: they did not consult for the World Bank, and they did not write *longue-durée* history designed to be consumed by the leaders of governmen-tal institutions. As historians, anthropologists, and sociologists stopped writing and working for the institutions of world govern-ment, economists took their place. Beyond history departments, the consequences of losing this audience of influential organisations has expressed itself in many other ways. A creeping science-envy within the social sciences more generally, leading to modelling; a focus on game-theory and rational actors – in short, a retreat to the individual and the abstract, not the collective and the concrete. A policy-driven focus on case-method migrated from law schools (where it had been established in the nineteenth century) to business schools and polit-ical science departments via the use of case-studies in medicine.[68] The baby-boom generation did much for the ability of historians to understand the world, but it did so at the cost of the ability of historians to speak back to the institutions of governance.

Seen in this light, a broad trend within anglophone historiography from the 1970s to the mid 2000s can be cast as evidence of a moral crisis, an inward-looking retreat from commenting on contemporary global issues and alternative futures. While historians refined their tools and their understandings of social justice, they simultaneously inflicted upon their discipline habits of microscopic attention that culminated in a sense of practical irrelevance, of the historian as astronomer in a high tower, distanced from a political and economic landscape. Part of this crisis was an increasing reluctance on the part of historians to enter the fray of international relations and public policy in the role of professional advisor. Instead, the role of advising citizens and policy-makers on the utopian possibilities of long-term change was largely ceded to colleagues in Economics departments, with the resulting dominance of newspaper headlines and policy circles by theories that idealise the free market, taking little to nothing from the moral lessons that postcolonial and social historians have drawn from the histories of empire and industrialisation, public health and the environment.[69]

By the 1990s, academic commentators in the United States complained about the increasing irrelevance of history and other humanities disciplines and looked nostalgically back to the New York intelligentsia of the 1950s and the active role played by historians and literary critics in the public sphere.[70] It looked to many colleagues as if the humanities had simply abandoned the public altogether. By the end of that decade, a younger generation of historians, just under the cusp of the baby-boom, began to reopen the question of the *longue durée*. Many of them were ancient and medieval historians by training, for whom silence on the topic of long time spans was perhaps particularly painful. For example, medievalist Daniel Lord Smail has led the charge into a dialogue with evolutionary biology, opening up questions about the periodisation of human identity and consumerism, among other topics.[71]

The moral stakes of *longue-durée* subjects – including the reorientation of our economy to cope with global warming and the integration of subaltern experience into policy – mandates that historians choose as large an audience as possible for all of the human experiences about which historians write – including (but not limited to) problems of environment, governance, capitalism, and exploitation. *Longue-durée* history is rightly deployed to allude to the Anthropocene when it becomes necessary to persuade an audience of the fact of a long-term relationship between humanity and the planet, and in particular to the atmosphere, delicate ecosystems, and constrained natural resources. But it may equally persuade us of the long struggles about the legacy of capitalism towards injustice, as did Tawney and Mumford, or over the governance of the environment.[72]

The return of the *longue durée* is intimately connected to changing questions of scale. In a moment of ever-growing inequality, amid crises of global governance, and under the impact of anthropogenic climate change, even a minimal understanding of the conditions shaping our lives demands a scaling-up of our inquiries. As the *longue durée* returns, in a new guise with new goals, it still demands a response to the most basic issues of historical methodology – of what problems we select, how we choose the boundaries of our topic, and what tools we put to solving the question. The power of memory can return us directly to the forgotten powers of history as a discipline to persuade, to reimagine, and to inspire. Renaissance historian Constantin Fasolt has argued that thinking about early modern civic institutions was largely premised on what he calls an attitude of 'historical revolt'.[73] In light of this, the new historians of the *longue durée* should be inspired to use history to criticise the institutions around us and to return history to its mission as a critical social science. History can provide the basis for a rejection of anachronisms founded on deference to longevity alone. Thinking with history – but only with long stretches of that history – may help us to choose which institutions to bury as dead and which we might want to keep alive.

*****

In the last decade, evidence for the return of the *longue durée* can be found across the intellectual landscape. A Latin Americanist notes of his field that 'it became unfashionable to posit theories about ... historical trajectories over the very long-run', but change is now in the air: 'Now the *longue durée* is back.' A European cultural historian tells his colleagues at a conference, 'all of us are ... invested, more or less explicitly, in a *longue durée* of sexuality'. And a professor of American Studies remarks of her discipline, 'Anyone in literary studies who has looked recently at titles of books, conferences, research clusters, and even syllabi across the field cannot have missed two key words ... that are doing substantial periodizing duty for literary and cultural criticism': one is geographical (the Atlantic world), the other 'a chronological unit, the *longue durée*'.[74] Recent works have placed the Cold War and migration, the Black Sea and the Arab Spring, women's spirituality and the history of Austria, German orientalism and concepts of empire, into the perspective of the *longue durée*.[75] And even a cursory scan of recent arrivals on the history bookshelves turns up a host of long-range histories, of around-the-world travel over 500 years; of the first 3,000 years of Christianity and of anti-Judaism from ancient Egypt to today; of strategy from chimpanzees to game theory, of genocide 'from Sparta to Darfur' and guerrilla warfare 'from ancient times to the present'; of the very 'shape' of human history over the last 15,000 years; and of a host of similar grand topics directed to wide reading publics.[76]

Indeed, big is back across a spectrum of new and revived modes of historical writing. Grandest of all is 'Big History', an account of the past stretching back to the origins of the universe itself.[77] More modest in scope, because it includes only the human past, is the still remarkably expansive 'Deep History' which spans some 40,000 years and deliberately breaks through the entrenched boundary between 'history' and 'pre-history'.[78] And more focused still, yet with perhaps the most immediate resonance for present concerns, is the history of the Anthropocene, the period in which human beings have comprised a collective actor powerful enough to affect the environment on a planetary scale.[79] The time-scales of these movements are, respectively, cosmological, archaeological, and climatological: each represents a novel expansion of historical perspectives, and each operates on horizons longer – usually much longer – than a generation, a human lifetime, or the other roughly biological time-spans that have defined most recent historical writing.

In this new work, contemporary historians are restoring the tight-woven cloak of stories that helps to shelter a culture with a sophisticated understanding of its past. A contemporary historian has recently urged 'that by returning to the macro-questions that shaped our discipline we can recapture its explanatory ambitions from the navel gazing of microhistories and in the process reestablish an understanding of the public utility of our work'.[80] History, with its rich, material understanding of human experience and institutions and its apprehension of multiple causality, is reentering the arena of long-term discussions of time where evolutionary biologists, archaeologists, climate scientists, and economists have long been the only protagonists. Today, we desperately need an arbiter for these mythological histories, capable of casting out prejudice, reestablishing consensus about the actual boundaries of the possible, and in so doing opening up a wider future and destiny for modern civilisations. History as a discipline can be that referee.

CHAPTER 4

Big questions, big data

One of the reasons that a society discovers itself in a crisis of long-term thinking is the problem of information overload. Information overload is not a new story in and of itself. European humanists in the Renaissance experienced it, as new editions of classical texts, new histories and chronology, and new information about the botany and fauna of Asia and the Americas rapidly swamped the abilities of scholars to aggregate information into encompassing theories or useful schedules. Indeed, many of our basic tools for search and retrieval – the index, the encyclopaedia, and the bibliography – came from the first era of information overload, when societies were feeling overwhelmed about their abilities to synthesise the past and peer into the future.[1]

We live in a new era of 'big data', from the decoding of the human genome to the billions of words of official reports annually churned out by government offices. In the social sciences and humanities big data have come to stand in for the aspiration of sociologists and historians to continued relevance, as our calculations open new possibilities for solving old questions and posing new ones.[2] Big data tend to drive the social sciences towards larger and larger problems, which in history are largely those of world events and institutional development over longer and longer periods of time. Projects about the long history of climate change, the consequences of the slave trade, or the varieties and fates of western property law make use of computational techniques, in ways that simultaneously pioneer new frontiers of data manipulation and make historical questions relevant to modern concerns.[3]

Over the last decade, the emergence of the digital humanities as a field has meant that a range of tools are within the grasp of anyone, scholar or citizen, who wants to try their hand at making sense of long stretches of time. Topic-modelling software can machine-read through millions of government or scientific reports and give back some basic facts about how our interests and ideas have changed over decades and centuries. Compellingly, many of these tools have the power of reducing to a small visualisation an archive of data otherwise too big to read. In our own time, many analysts are beginning to realise that in order to hold persuasive power, they need to condense big data in such a way that they can circulate among readers as a concise story that is easy to tell.

While humanity has experimented with drawing timelines for centuries, reducing the big picture to a visualisation is made newly possible by the increasing availability of big data.[4] That in turn raises the pressing questions of whether we go long or short with that data. There are places in the historical record where that decision – to look at a wider context or not – makes all the difference in the world. The need to frame questions more and more broadly determines which data we use and how we manipulate it, a challenge that much *longue-durée* work has yet to take up. Big data enhance our ability to grapple with historical information. They may help us to decide the hierarchy of causality – which events mark watershed moments in their history, and which are merely part of a larger pattern.

NEW TOOLS

In the second decade of the twenty-first century, digitally based keyword search began to appear everywhere as a basis for scholarly inquiry. In the era of digitised knowledge banks, the basic tools for analysing social change around us are everywhere. The habits of using keyword search to expand coverage of historical change over large time-scales appeared in political science and linguistics journals, analysing topics as diverse as the pubic reaction to genetically modified corn in Gujarat, the reception of climate change science in UK newspapers, the representation of Chinese peasants in the western press, the persistence of anti-semitism in British culture, the history of public housing policy, and the fate of attempts by the British coal industry to adapt to pollution regulations.[5] In 2011 and 2013, social scientists trying to analyse the relationship between academic publications about climate and public opinion resorted to searching the Web of Science database for simple text strings like 'global warming' and 'global climate change', then ranking the articles they found by their endorsement of various positions.[6] In short, new technologies for analysing digitised databases drove a plurality of studies that aggregate information about discourses and social communities over time, but few of these studies were published in mainstream history journals.[7] There was a disconnection between technologies clearly able to measure aggregate transformations of discourses over decades, and the ability, the willingness, or even the courage of history students to measure these questions for themselves.

To overcome this resistance, new tools created for *longue-durée* historical research, and specifically designed to deal with the proliferation of government data in our time, have become an ever more-pressing necessity. Here we give one example, drawn from Jo Guldi's experience, of how the challenges of question-driven research on new bodies of data led to the creation of a new tool. In the summer of 2012, she led a team of researchers that released Paper Machines, a digital toolkit designed to help scholars parse the massive amounts of paper involved in any comprehensive, international look at the over-documented twentieth century. Paper Machines is an open-source extension of Zotero – a program that allows users to create bibliographies and build their own hand-curated libraries in an online database – designed with the range of historians' textual sources in mind.[8] Its purpose is to make state-of-the-art text mining accessible to scholars across a variety of disciplines in the humanities and social sciences who lack extensive technical knowledge or immense computational resources.

While tool sets like Google Books Ngram Viewer utilise preset corpora from Google Book Search that automatically emphasise the Anglo-American tradition, Paper Machines works with the individual researcher's own hand-tailored collections of texts, whether mined from digital sources like newspapers and chat rooms or scanned and saved through optical character recognition (OCR) from paper sources like government archives. It can allow a class, a group of scholars, or scholars and activists together to collect and share archives of texts. These group libraries can be set as public or private depending on the sensitivity and copyright restrictions of the material being collected: historians of Panama have used a Zotero group library to collect and share the texts of government libraries for which no official finding aid exists. The scholars themselves are thus engaged in preserving, annotating, and making discoverable historical resources that otherwise risk neglect, decay, or even intentional damage.

With Paper Machines, scholars can create visual representations of a multitude of patterns within a text corpus using a simple, easy-to-use graphical interface. One may use the tool to generalise about a wide body of thought – for instance, things historians have said in a particular journal over the last ten years. Or one may visualise libraries against each other – say, novels about nineteenth-century London set against novels about nineteenth-century Paris. Using this tool, a multitude of patterns in text can be rendered visible through a simple graphical interface. Applying Paper Machines to text corpora allows scholars to accumulate hypotheses about *longue-durée* patterns in the influence of ideas, individuals, and professional cohorts.

By measuring trends, ideas, and institutions against each other over time, scholars will be able to take on a much larger body of texts than they normally do. For example, in applying Paper Machines to a hand-curated text corpus of large numbers of bureaucratic texts on global land reform from the twentieth century, it has been possible to trace the conversations in British history from the local stories at their points of origin forward, leaping from micro-historical research in British archives into a *longue-durée* synthesis of policy trends on a worldwide scale. That digitally enabled research operates through a threefold process: digitally synthesising broad swathes of time, critically inquiring into the micro-historical archive with digit-ally informed discernment about which archives to choose, and reading more broadly in secondary literatures from adjacent fields. For example, in Figure 4, the topic-modelling algorithm MALLET has been run on a corpus of scholarly texts about land law. The resulting image is a computer-guided timeline of the relative prom-inence of ideas – some mentioning Ireland and some mentioning India – that can then be changed and fine-tuned. This visualisation of changing concepts over time guides the historian to look more closely in her corpus at the 1950s and 1960s, when the intellectual memory of land struggles in Ireland was helping to guide contem-porary policy in Latin America.

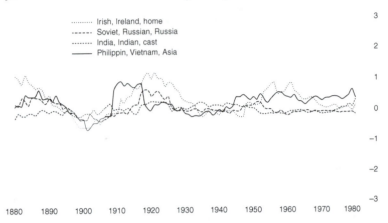

Figure 4 Relative prominence of mentions of India, Ireland, and other topics in relationship to each other, 1880–1980. (Thin lines indicate fewer documents upon which to base analysis.) *Source*: Paper Machines, employing MALLET, topic-modelling software by David Mimno.

This digitally driven research provides the basis for Guldi's *The Long Land War*, a historical monograph telling the story of the global progress of land reform movements, tracing ideas about worker allotments and food security, participatory governance, and rent control from the height of the British Empire to the present.[9] Paper Machines has synthesised the nature of particular debates and their geographic referents, making for instance timelines and spatial maps of topics and place-names associated with rent control, land reform, and allotment gardening. It has also shown which archives to choose and which parts of those archives to focus upon. Paper Machines was designed as a tool for hacking bureaucracies, for forming a portrait of their workings, giving an immediate context to documents from the archive. The user of Paper Machines can afford to pay attention to the field agents, branch heads, and directors-general of UN offices, or indeed to the intermediate faculty of the University of Wisconsin and the University of Sussex who offered advice to both bureaucrats and generations of undergraduates. The tool allows us to instantly take the measure of each of these organs, identifying the ways in which they diverge and converge. All of their staff spoke a common language of modernisation theory: of national governments, democratic reform, government-provided extension, training and management, and the provision of new equipment that resulted in quantitatively verifiable increased production.

Traditional research, limited by the sheer breadth of the non-digitised archive and the time necessary to sort through it, becomes easily shackled to histories of institutions and actors in power, for instance characterising universal trends in the American empire from the Ford and Rockefeller Foundations' investments in pesticides, as some historians have done. By identifying vying topics over time, Paper Machines allows the reader to identify and pursue particular moments of dissent, schism, and utopianism – zeroing in on conflicts between the pesticide industry and the Appropriate Technology movement or between the World Bank and the Liberation Theology movement over exploitative practices, for example. Digitally structured reading means giving more time to counterfactuals and suppressed voices, realigning the archive to the intentions of history from below.

Other similar tools can offer metrics for understanding long-term changes over history from the banal to the profound. Google Ngrams offers a rough guide to the rise and fall of ideas.[10] Humanists like Franco Moretti and historians like Ben Schmidt have been crucial collaborators in the design of tools for visualisation over time, in Moretti's case collaborating with IBM to produce the ManyEyes software for 'distant reading' of large bodies of text; in Schmidt's case, working alongside the genetic biologists who coded the software behind Google Ngrams to ensure that the software produced reliable timelines of the textual dominance of certain words from generation to generation.[11]

Tools such as these lend themselves to scholars looking to measure aggregate changes over decades and centuries. The arrival in the past ten years of mass digitisation projects in libraries and crowd-sourced oral histories online announced an age of easy access to a tremendous amount of archival material. Coupled with the constructive use of tools for abstracting knowledge, these digital corpora invite scholars to try out historical hypotheses across the time-scale of centuries.[12] The nature of the tools available and the abundance of texts render history that is both *longue durée* and simultaneously archival a surmountable problem, at least for post-classical Latin – a corpus 'arguably span[ning] the greatest historical distance of any major textual collection today' – and for sources in major European languages created since the Renaissance.[13]

Tools for comparing quantitative information have come to question standard narratives of modernity. For Michael Friendly, data visualisation has made possible revisiting old theories of political economy with the best of current data on the experience of the past, for instance, using up-to-date data to recreate William Playfair's famous time series graph showing the ratio of the price of wheat to wages in the era of the Napoleonic Wars. Friendly has proposed that historians turn to the accumulation of as many measures of happiness, nutrition, population, and governance as possible, and become experts at the comparative modelling of multiple variables over time.[14] These skills would also make history into an arbiter of mainline discourses about the Anthropocene, experience, and institutions.

In law and other forms of institutional history, where the premium on precedent gives *longue-durée* answers a peculiar power, there will be more of such work sooner rather than later. New tools that expand the individual historian's ability to synthesise such large amounts of information open the door to moral impulses that already exist elsewhere in the discipline of history, impulses to examine the horizon of possible conversations about governance over the *longue durée*. Scholars working on the history of European law have found that digital methods enable them to answer questions of longer scale: for example, the Old Bailey Online, covering English cases from the period 1673 to 1914 – the largest collection of subaltern sources now available in the English-speaking world; or Colin Wilder's 'Republic of Literature' project which, by digitising early-modern legal texts and linking the text-based information to a gigantic social networking map of teachers and students of law, aims to show who drove legal change in early modern Germany, where many of our first ideas of the public domain, private property, and mutuality emerged.[15] Projects of this kind offer a tantalising grip on the kind of multi-researcher questions, extending across time and space which, by aggregating information on a scale hitherto unknown, may help to transform our understanding of the history of laws and society.

In the new era of digital analysis, the watchword of the fundable project must be *extensibility* – will this dataset work with other forms of infrastructure? Will these texts help us to tell the long story, the big story – to fill in the gaps left by Google Books? Or is this a single exhibition, which can only be appreciated by the scholar absorbed in reflection about a decade or two? Will students scramble to get the text in a format which the tools of digital analysis can make sense of?

Long-term thinkers frequently avoid engaging digital tools for analysing the big picture. The new *longue durée*-ists might have been expected to step into this role of carefully analysing the data of many disciplines, as their stories synthesise and interweave narratives borrowed from other places. But they have often shied away from big data; they generally prefer to construct traditional synthetic narratives by way of secondary sources. When there is such a mismatch between goals and resources, there may yet be opportunities for more ambitious work on a larger scale. Some have heard the clarion call to return to the big picture, and some have responded to the promise of the digital toolkit. But few have used the two together, applying tools designed to analyse large troves of resources to questions about our long-term past and long-term future.

THE RISE OF BIG DATA

In the six decades since the Second World War, the natural and the human sciences have accumulated immense troves of quantifiable data which is rarely put side by side. The rise of public debate has driven the availability of more and more time-designated data, which have been made available in interchangeable formats by governments, climate scientists, and other entities. The world needs authorities capable of talking rationally about the data in which we all swim, their use, abuse, abstraction, and synthesis. Such data have been accumulated over decades of research supporting new theses, for instance, the academic consensus on climate change. Big data have been steadily accumulating from all quarters since the first ice-cores were drilled in the 1960s and computer-based models have extended the data collected around meteorology into possible suggestions about how our atmosphere was changing in relationship to pollution.[16]

In history journals, these datasets have so far had relatively little impact, but in nearby fields, scientists of climate and atmosphere have tabulated global datasets for the twentieth century, a portrait of planetary droughts and floods as they increased over the century.[17] Particular studies model how farms and farmers in Switzerland, the Netherlands, or the Atlantic coast of the United States have responded over the course of centuries to vanishing wetlands, surging floods, and changing maize or other crop yields influenced by rising temperatures.[18] They have even experimented with datasets that correlate a range of cultural and social responses in history to moments of global climate change.[19] An article in the journal *Environmental Innovation and Societal Transitions* compares social complexity, food production, and leisure time over the last 12,000 years to the prospect of technological innovation to come, and takes information even from the fall of Rome. Climate change has been offered as evidence for China's century-long cycles of war and peace over millennia, for the 'General Crisis' of the seventeenth century, and as the original cause of the civil war in Darfur.[20] As a result of the accumulation of data about our deep atmospheric past, the past of the environment now appears provocatively human in its outward aspect.

Once one starts to look, the untapped sources of historical data are everywhere. Government offices collect long time-span assessments of energy, climate, and the economy. The US Energy Information Administration publishes a *Monthly Energy Review* going back as far as 1949. These tables of energy consumption have been analysed by climate scientists, but much less frequently by historians. Official data on population, government balance of payments, foreign debt, interest and exchange rates, money supply, and employment are collected from world governments and made available to scholars by international governance bodies like UNdata and Euromonitor International and by private databases like IHS Global Insight. The IMF has collected finance statistics for every government in the world from 1972.[21] Government data collected over long-time scales have been analysed in sociology, climate science, and economics.[22] These streams of data have traditionally been less frequently taken advantage of by historians, but that may be changing. As historians begin to look at longer and longer time-scales, quantitative data collected by governments over the centuries begin to offer important metrics for showing how the experiences of community and opportunity can change from one generation to the next.

There is a superabundance of quantitative data available in our time, material that was hardly available if at all in the 1970s, when history last had a quantitative turn. The historian working today can work with maps that layer atop each other decades if not centuries of international trade routes, population growth, average income, rainfall, and weather.[23] She can leaf through an atlas of the international slave trade based on one of the great digital projects over the *longue durée*, the Trans-Atlantic Slave Trade Database which accumulates information on some 35,000 slave voyages from the sixteenth century to the nineteenth century carrying over 12 million enslaved people.[24] Using Google Earth, she can peel back transparencies made from sixteenth- to nineteenth-century maps showing London's growth. For any study, big or small, the data that form a background to our work now abound.

Very little of the data that have been accumulated in this time has yet been interpreted. The information age – first named as such in 1962, and defined as the era when governments regularly monitored their populations and environments, collecting data on soil erosion, weather, population, and employment – has resulted, as of the twenty-first century, in the accumulation of historically deep data.[25] Collected frequently enough over time, those numbers sketch the shape of changing history, changing contexts of consequences – the whole of which are rarely put together by observers inside the disciplines. These quantitative data have begun to superabound, offering rich frontiers for a new school of quantitative analysis. Yet much of that data has only been assessed in the moment, over the short time-scale of economic findings about recent trends.

The first flickering of a revolution in using macroscopic data to look at the big picture is beginning to show on the horizons of some of the world's research universities, where interest in government-collected data has prompted a resurgence of cliometrics, which refers to the study of History (embodied by the Greek muse, Clio) through the history of things that can be quantitatively measured – wealth, goods, and services that were taxed and recorded, and population. That school was first in vogue in the 1970s, when economic historians like Robert Fogel and Stanley Engerman compared the poor nutrition of mill-labourers in the American north and slaves in the American South, using those numbers to argue that capitalism was actually *worse than slavery* for the victims of a society in terms of how much food a worker and a slave consumed. There was a lot to be said about Fogel's and Engerman's numbers, and about any sense in which slavery could be considered 'better' or 'more rational' than the market, and perhaps for the reasons of this confusion of argument, cliometrics afterwards disappeared.[26] The micro-history that triumphed in those debates was, as we have seen, if anything over-fastidious in its interpretation of first-person experiences as a guide to the interpretation of slavery as well as capitalism. Banished for its sins, cliometrics has not been part of the graduate training of most students of history or in economics for some time now. But in a new era of big data, the evidence available is richer and aggregated from more institutions than before.

The counting of things that can be measured as a guide to doing history is now back in abundance, and with greater sensitivity to questions of class, race, identity, and authority than ever before. Following in the path of an older quantitative turn, data-driven historians like Christopher Dyer have returned to the use of probate records from late medieval England to demonstrate an ethos of care for the poor and sustaining the common good.[27] When historian Thomas Maloney set out to learn the impact of racism on unemployed men during the Great Depression, he turned to forgotten troves of government data as well. Government records on selective service integrated with employment records allowed him to measure trends in Cincinnati over two decades, and to learn that men who lived in segregated neighbourhoods actually fared better than those on the verge of integration.[28] Questions such as these illuminate the way in which a new quantitative turn is adding subtleties of racial experience and belonging, all theorised under a micro-historical turn linked to the availability of long-run datasets.

Outside history departments, however, the ambitions attached to these datasets are of much greater scale. Since the 1970s, non-profit think-tanks like Freedom House, The International Research and Exchanges Board (IREX), and the Rand Corporation have subsidised the efforts of political scientists to put together databanks that track characteristics like 'peace' and 'conflict', 'democracy' and 'authoritarianism', or 'freedom of the press' and 'human rights' across the nations of the world.[29] Since the late 1990s, some of these datasets have incorporated information about time, tracking collections of events related to the expansion of rights, reaching back to 1800 and forward up to the present.[30] While some of these datasets are personal or proprietary, others are available for sharing, and this sharing has generated innovation in the way we understand these variables. Big data can also push historical insight into the nature of inequality. Economic historians and sociologists are already tracking inequality over centuries and across nations, searching for the patterns of belonging, and preliminary studies have begun to demonstrate the wide variability in the experience of men and women, blacks and whites, migrants and stationary people across large timescales as well.[31]

The richness of so much data on the long term raises important methodological issues of how much background any scholar should possess to understand a particular moment in time. When mapped against histories of weather, trade, agricultural production, food consumption, and other material realities, the environment interweaves with human conditions. Layering known patterns of reality upon each other produces startling indicators of how the world has changed – for instance, the concentration of aerosols identified from the mid twentieth century in parts of India has been proven to have disrupted the pattern of the monsoon in the latter part of the twentieth century.[32] Maps that layer environmental disturbances and human events onto each other already reveal how humans are responding to global warming and rising sea-levels. In parts of the Netherlands, rising waters had already begun to shift the pattern of agricultural cultivation two hundred years ago.[33] By placing government data about farms next to data on the weather, history allows us to see the interplay of material change with human experience, and how a changing climate has already been creating different sets of winners and losers over decades.

The implications of these studies are immense. Even before the advent of big data, in 1981 Amartya Sen had already established a correlation between higher levels of democracy and averting famines.[34] But more recently scholars dealing with big data have used historical indexes of democracy and WHO-provided indexes of disease, life expectancy, and infant mortality to establish a pattern that links democracy to health in most nations' experience over the course of the twentieth century.[35] Different kinds of data provide correlations that evince the shape of the good life, demonstrating how societies' relationships with particular health conditions change dramatically over a century.[36] The data also suggest how different the experience of history can be from one part of the world to the next, as in the farming regions where agricultural productivity produced a generation of short adults, marked for the rest of their life by malnourishment.[37] Aggregated historically across time and space, in this way big data can mark out the hazards of inequality, and the reality of systems of governance and market that sustain life for all.

What all of this work proves is that we are awash in data – data about democracy, health, wealth, and ecology; data of many sorts. Data that are assessed, according to the old scheme of things, appears in several different departments – democracy in political science or international relations; wealth in sociology or anthropology; and ecology in earth science or evolutionary biology. But data scientists everywhere are starting to understand that data of different kinds must be understood in their historical relationship. Aerosol pollution and the changing monsoon have a causal relationship. So do rising sea-levels and the migration of farmers. All of the data are unified by interaction over time. Creative manipulation of archives of this kind give us data unglimpsed by most economists and climate scientists. When data are expanded, critiqued, and examined historically from multiple points of view, ever more revealing correlations become possible.

INVISIBLE ARCHIVES

One of the particular tricks of the historian is to peer into the cabinet of papers marked 'DO NOT READ', to become curious about what the official mind has masked. This tactic, too, is gaining new life in an era of big data. Rich information can help to illuminate the deliberate silences in the archive, shining the light onto parts of the government that some would rather the public not see. These are the Dark Archives, archives that do not just wait around for the researcher to visit, but which rather have to be built by reading what has been declassified or removed. Here, too, big data can help to tell a longer, deeper story of how much has disappeared, when, and why.

In the task of expanding the archive in ways that destabilise power, historians are taking the lead. Historian Matthew Connelly devised a website which he calls a 'Declassification Engine', designed for helping the public to trace unpublished or undocumented US Department of State reports. The techniques he has used should make it possible to perform a distant reading of reports that were never even publicly released. In fact, his research has revealed an enormous increase in declassified files since the 1990s. Rather than classifying specific files understood to be deeply sensitive because of individuals or projects named therein, in the 1990s the US government began to automatically withhold entire state programmes from public access. By crowd-sourcing the rejection of requests for Freedom of Information Acts, Connelly's Declassification Engine was able to show the decades-long silencing of the archives.[38]

In the era of the NGO, government-sourced data streams have been supplemented by multiple other datasets of human experience and institutions over time, made possible by the crowd-sourcing power of the Internet. The use of the Internet for collecting and sharing data from various sources has also given rise to the bundling of new collections of data by non-governmental activist groups monitoring the path of capitalism. Indeed, social scientists have been compiling their own datasets for generations, but since the 1990s many of those datasets have been computerised and even shareable.[39] The result is a generation of databases critical of both nation-states and corporations, which give evidence for alternative histories of the present. In 2012, four German research universities banded together with the International Land Coalition to begin collecting information on the nearly invisible 'land grab' happening across the world as a result of the mobilisation of finance capital.[40] In the era of data, we can make visible even those histories that both the state and investors would rather we not tell.

What is true of the International Land Coalition is likely true for many groups: in an age of big data, one activist stance is to collect information on a phenomenon invisible to traditional governments, and to use those data as themselves a tool for international reform. Similar activist databases exist in Wikileaks, the famous trove of whistle-blower-released national papers, and Offshoreleaks, in the context of tax havens, those international sites for individuals and corporations diverting their profits from nation-states, for which journalist Nicholas Shaxson has written a preliminary history of the twentieth century in his *Treasure Islands* (2011).[41]

For the moment, the data collected in banks such as these only cover a short historical spectrum, but it begs for supplementation by historians capable of tracing foreign investment in postcolonial real estate – a subject that would look backwards at the history of resource nationalism in the 1940s and 1950s, and at the sudden reversal in the recent decade of these laws, as nations like Romania, Bulgaria, and Iceland open their real estate to international speculation for the first time in a half-century.

Dark Archives and community-built archives dramatise how much big data can offer us in terms of a portrait of the present – what our government looks like now, where investment is moving, and what is the fate of social justice today. Combined with other kinds of tools for analysing the past, including the topic modelling and other tools we discussed above, digital analysis begins to offer an immense toolset for handling history when there is simply too much paper to read. We are no longer in the age of information overload; we are in an era when new tools and sources are beginning to sketch in the immense stretches of time that were previously passed over in silence.

Evidence of displacement and suppression needs to be kept. It is the most fragile and the most likely to perish in any economic, political, or environmental struggle. A few years ago, biodiversity activists in England erected a memorial to the lost species, known and unknown, which perished because of human-caused climate change.[42] Even old archives can be suddenly repurposed to illuminating big stories about extinction events, as with the eighteenth-century natural history collections gathered by naturalists working for the East India Company and others that have been used by ecologists to reconstruct the pattern of extinctions that characterised the Anthropocene.[43] We need libraries populated with information on plants, animals, and also indigenous peoples and evicted or forgotten peoples, the raw data for Dark Archives of stories that it would be only too convenient to forget. Preservation and reconstruction of datasets in the name of larger ethical challenges poses a worthy challenge for historians of science. They will give us a richer, more participatory picture of the many individuals who experience economic inequality and environmental devastation, of the many hands that have wrought democracy and brought about the 'modern' world.

As we have seen, those tools for illuminating the past frequently reverberate back on our understanding of the future: they change how we understand the possibilities of sustainable city building, or inequality over the last few centuries; they help activists and citizens to understand the trajectory of their government, and how to interpret the world economy. All of these means of doing history are also crucial for making sense of world events in present time, and they represent an emerging technology for modelling the background for a long-term future.

HOW THEN SHOULD WE THINK ABOUT THE FUTURE AND THE PAST?

Digitisation by itself is not sufficient to break through the fog of stories and the confusion of a society divided by competing mythologies. Cautious and judicious curating of possible data, questions, and subjects is necessary. We must strive to discern and promote questions that are synthetic and relevant and which break new methodological ground. Indeed, the ability to make sense of causal questions, to tell persuasive stories over time, is one of the unresolved challenges facing the information industry today. Famously, neither Google nor Facebook has had much success in finding an algorithm that will give the reader the single *most* important news story from their wall or from the magazines over the last year. They can count the most *viewed* story, but the question of the most influential has challenged them. Experimenting with timelines that would make sense of complex real-world events, Tarikh Korula of TechCrunch and Mor Naaman of Cornell University have produced a website called Seen.co, which charts in real time the relative 'heat' of different hashtags on Twitter.[44] This enterprise points to the hunger in the private sector for experts who understand time – on either the short *durée* or the long. Similarly, another event-tracking site, Recorded Future, finds synchronicities and connections between stories, concentrating around particular companies or investment sectors, with a client base of intelligence and corporate arbitrage.[45] Its CEO,

Christopher Ahlberg, describes its mission as ' help[ing] people [to] see all kinds of new stories and structures in the world'.[46] The skill of noticing patterns in events, finding corrrelations and connections – all the bailiwick of traditional history – was held by Google to be such a worthwhile venture that the reported initial investment in the company in 2014 was tagged at $8 billion.

The life of the Paper Machines software offers another illustration. Paper Machines was created in 2012 and refined through 2013–14, producing a small number of papers and a large number of blog entries and tweets by faculty and graduate students reflecting on their experience in using it in pedagogy and research. By 2013, however, it had also been adopted by a military intelligence firm in Denmark, advising Danish national intelligence about the nature of official reports from other world intelligence forces.[47] Those governments, much like the historical governments that Paper Machines was designed to study, produce too much paper to read – indeed, too much intelligence for other national governments to make useful sense of it. Identifying historical trends that concerned different national security forces turned out to be vital to the efficient process-ing of official information.

In the decades to come, the best tools for modelling time will be sought out by data scientists, climate scientists, visualisation experts, and the finance sector. History has an important role to play in developing standards, techniques, and theories suited to the analy-sis of mutually incompatible datasets where a temporal element is crucial to making sense of causation and correlation. Experts trying to explain the history and prospects of various insurance, real-estate, manufacturing, ecological, or political programmes to potential share-holders all need experts in asking questions that scale over time. All of these potential audiences also raise concerns, for many historians, of the moral implications of forms of history that evolve to answer real-world and practical problems.

HOW THE AGE OF BIG DATA WILL CHANGE THE UNIVERSITY

The scale of information overload is a reality of the knowledge economy in our time. Digital archives and toolsets promise to make sense of government and corporate data that currently overwhelm the abilities of scholars, the media, and citizens. The immensity of the material in front of us begs for arbitrators who can help make sense of data that defy the boundaries of expertise – data that are at once economic, ecological, and political in nature, and that were collected in the past by institutions whose purposes and biases have changed over time. Big data will almost certainly change the functions of the university. We believe that the university of the future needs not only more data and greater mathematical rigour, but also greater arbitration of the data that were collected over time.

There are still reasons to think that a university education is the proper site for long-term research into the past and future, and that such an education should be in high demand at a moment when climates, economies, and governments are experiencing so much flux. The university offers a crucial space for reflection in the lives of individuals and societies. In a world of mobility, the university's long sense of historical traditions substitutes for the long-term thinking that was the preserve of shamans, priests, and elders in another community. We need that orientation to time insofar as we too want to engage the past in order to better explore the future.

Many of the experts in the modern university are nonetheless ill equipped to handle questions such as these. Even on shorter scales, scientists trained to work with data can sometimes err when they begin to work with big data that were accrued by human institutions working over time. A paper by geographers tried to answer the question of whether the public was responding to data about climate change by keyword searching the ISI Web of Knowledge database for the key topic terms 'climat* chang*' and 'adapt*'.[48] Does a word-count of this kind really pass on information about climate change as a rising priority in America? A strategy such as this would never pass muster in a history journal. As we have shown in Chapter 3, even a mountain of evidence about climate change collected by scientists is no indication of public consensus in the world outside the academy. But even on a much more fine-grained level, the analysis described in this project is problematic. Even the strings chosen exclude discourse-dependent variations like 'global warming' and 'environmental change'. Still more importantly, discussion of adaptation among academics is hardly a metric of political action in the outside world.

Even more telling is the case of the data that Americans use to talk about the past and future of unemployment. This measure of national economic well-being circulates among political scientists, economics, and the international media as shorthand for what is politically desirable as a goal for us all. But according to Zachary Karabell, a financial analyst as well as an accredited historian of the indicators with which we measure our society, the way we use the measure of unemployment itself is laden with the biases of short-term thinking. Unemployment excludes many kinds of work from its count, which was originally developed under the New Deal, and true to the biases of its time excludes from the category of 'employment' every time an urban farmer starts up a project and all household labour performed by women who have opted to take care of their children or parents rather than seeking employment in the workforce. It also represents a peculiarly short-term horizon for measuring economic well-being or certain goals. Because no institution offered a statistic for 'unemployment' of a kind commensurate with our own measure before 1959, many 'supposed truisms' of success and failure in a presidential election turn out to be false, writes Karabell. These accepted truisms including the belief, repeated in nearly every electoral cycle, that no American president can be reelected with an unemployment rate above 7.2 per cent. Such fictions 'are based on barely more than fifty years of information', writes Karabell. That time horizon, this historian shows, is 'hardly a blip in time and not nearly enough to make hard and fast conclusions with any certainty'.[49]

In almost every institution that collects data over time, the way those data are collected is refined and changed from one generation to the next. When Freedom House, the NGO founded in 1941, began collecting datasets on peace, conflict, and democratisation, the metrics it used stressed freedom of the press; a very different standard from the Polity Project's measures of democracy and autocracy in terms of institutions, developed decades later. Those shifting values in political science mean that the Freedom House and Polity metrics of democracy are both useful, albeit for different projects.[50] In other fields, however, the outmoding of measures can cause grave difficulties in the usefulness of data altogether. Not only are measures like employment, the consumer price index (CPI), inflation, or gross domestic product (GDP) calculated on the basis of the way we lived in the era before the microwave oven, but also its theories and supposed laws may reflect enduring biases of old-world aristocrats and Presbyterian elders. According to Karabell, this is one reason why financial institutions in our era are abandoning traditional economic measures altogether, hiring mathematicians and historians to contrive 'bespoke indicators' that tell us more about the way we live now.[51]

We have been navigating the future by the numbers, but we may not have been paying sufficient attention to *when* the numbers come from. It is vital that an information society whose data come from different points in time has arbiters of information trained to work with time. Yet climatologists and economists nonetheless continue to analyse change over time and to take on big-picture questions of its meaning, including the collapse of civilisations like Rome or the Maya, usually without asking how much of our data about each came from elites denouncing democracy as the source of social breakdown or from later empires trumpeting their own victory.[52] In an age threatened by information overload, we need a historical interpretation of the data that swarm over us – both the official record of jobs, taxes, land, and water, and the unofficial record of Dark Archives, everyday experience, and suppressed voices.

WAR BETWEEN THE EXPERTS

The arbitration of data is a role in which the History departments of major research universities will almost certainly take a lead; it requires talents and training which no other discipline possesses. In part, this role consists of the special attachment to the interpretation of the past harboured by historians around the world. Many of the dilemmas about which data we look at are ethical questions that historians already understand. In an era when intelligence services, the finance sector, and activists might all hope to interpret the long and short events that make up our world, historians have much to offer. If History departments train designers of tools and analysts of big data, they stand to manufacture students on the cutting edge of knowledge-making within and beyond the academy.

History's particular tools for weighing data rest on several claims: noticing institutional bias in the data, thinking about where data come from, comparing data of different kinds, resisting the powerful pull of received mythology, and understanding that there are different kinds of causes. Historians have also been among the most important interpreters, critics, and sceptics investigating the way that 'the official mind' of bureaucracy collects and manages data from one generation to the next. The tradition of thinking about the past and future of data may lead back to Harold Perkin's history of the professions, or before that to Max Weber's work on the history of bureaucracy.[53] What their work has consistently shown is that the data of modern bureaucracy, science, and even mathematics is reliably aligned with the values of the institution that produced it. Sometimes that takes the form of bias on behalf of a particular region that funds most of the projects, as it did for the American Army Corps of Engineers. Sometimes it takes the form of bias on behalf of experts itself – bias that shows that the resources of the poor can never amount to much in a market economy; bias that suggests that economists are indispensable aids to growing the economy, even when most of their scholarship merely supports the concentration of already existing wealth in the hands of the few.[54] Historians are trained to look at the various kinds of data, even when they come from radically different sources. These are skills that are often overlooked in the training of other kinds of analysts; the reading of temporally generated sequences of heterogeneous data is a historian's speciality.

The critique of received mythology about history goes by the name of 'metanarratives'. Since the 1960s, much work in the theory and philosophy of history has concentrated on how a historian gains a critical perspective on the biases of earlier cultures, including the prejudice that Protestant, white, or European perspectives were always the most advanced. Scepticism towards universal rules of preferment is one vital tool for thinking about the past and the future. There is, so far as history can teach, no natural law that predicts the triumph of one race or religion over another, although there are smaller dynamics that correlate with the rise and fall of particular institutions at particular times, for example access to military technology and infrastructure on an unprecedented scale.[55] This scepticism sets historians aside from the fomenters of fundamentalisms about how democracy or American civilisation is destined to triumph over others.

We live in an age where big data seem to suggest that we are locked into our history, our path dependent on larger structures that arrived before we did. For example, 'Women and the Plough', an economics article in a prestigious journal, tells us that modern gender roles have structured our preferences since the institution of agriculture.[56] 'Was the Wealth of Nations Determined in 1000 BC?' asks another.[57] Evolutionary biology, much like economics, has also been a field where an abundance of data nevertheless has only been read towards one or two hypotheses about human agency. The blame is placed on humans as a species, or on agriculture, or on the discovery of fire. Our genes have been blamed for our systems of hierarchy and greed, for our gender roles, and for the exploitation of the planet itself. And yet gender roles and systems of hierarchy show enormous variations in human history.

When some scholars talk in this way of unchanging rules inherited from hunter-gatherer ancestors, they themselves may forget, persuaded by the bulk of accumulated evidence, that their theory, translated via Darwin and Malthus, remains at its core a philosophy which reasons that an unchanging earth gave to all of its creatures, humankind included, stable patterns of action, which they defied at their peril. In the world of the evolutionary biologist and neo-liberal economist, the possibility of choosing and curating multiple futures itself seems to disappear. These are reductionist fictions about our past and future merely masquerading as data-supported theories; the historian notices that they are also outmoded ones.

At other times, the repeated story instructs us about how to govern our society and deal with other people. When economists and political scientists talk about Malthusian limits to growth, and how we have passed the 'carrying capacity' of our planet, historians recognise that they are rehearsing not a proven fact, but a fundamentally theological argument. Modern economists have removed the picture of an abusive God from their theories, but their theory of history is still at root an early nineteenth-century one, where the universe is designed to punish the poor, and the experience of the rich is a sign of their obedience to natural laws.[58] Today, anthropologists can point to the evidence of many societies, past and present, where the divisions of class are not expressed in terms of ejectment or starvation.[59]

The reality of natural laws and the predominance of pattern do not bind individuals to any particular fate: within their grasp, there still remains an ability to choose, embodied in individual agency, which is one cause among many working to create the future. But this is not how many disciplines today reason. As Geoffrey Hodgson has concluded in his analyses of modern economics as a discipline, 'mainstream economics, by focusing on the concept of equilibrium, has neglected the problem of causality'. 'Today', Hodgson concludes, 'researchers concerned wholly with data-gathering, or mathematical model building, often seem unable to appreciate the underlying problems'.[60]

Outside of History departments, few scholars are trained to test the conclusions of their own field against conclusions forged on the other side of the university. Biologists deal with biology; economists with economics. But historians are almost always historians of something; they find themselves asking where the data came from – and wondering how good they are, even (or especially) if they came from another historian. In traditional history, multiple causality is embedded in the very structure of departments, such that a student of history gains experience of many possible aspects of history and its causation by taking classes in intellectual history, art history, or history of science – subjects that reflect a reality forged by many hands. Almost every historian today tends to fuse these tools together – they are a historian who deals with the *social* experience in an *ecological* context of *intellectual* ideas and *diplomatic* policy. In other words, if they treat the last two centuries, they are handling the recorded experience of working-class people, given an ecological disaster, and making a connection to what lawyers said and politicians did. These modern historians at least work, as historian James Vernon urges, 'to write a history of global modernity that is plural in cause and singular in condition'.[61] They are putting the data about inequality and policy and ecosystems on the same page, and reducing big noise to one causally complex story.[62]

In a world of big data, the world needs analysts who are trained in comparing discrete sets of incompatible data, quantitative and qualitative; words about emotions in court records; judging climate change against attitudes towards nature and its exploitation held by the official mind or the mind of the entrepreneur. Who can tell us about the differences between the kinds of rationality used in climate debates and the kinds of rationality used in talking about inequality? Are these stories really irreconcilable?

Without historians' theories of multiple causality, fundamentalism and dogmatism could prevail. In this diminished understanding of history, there can be barely more than one imaginable future. Because we are allegedly creatures predetermined by an ancient past, the story goes, our choices are either a future of environmental catastrophe or rule by self-appointed elites, whether biological or technological. By raising the question of how we have learned to think differently from our ancestors, we separate ourselves from uncritical use of data and theories that were collected by another generation for other purposes.[63]

Historians should be at the forefront of devising new methodologies for surveying social change on the aggregate level. At the very least, they should be comparing and contrasting keyword-enabled searches in journals, policy papers, and news against economic reports and climate data, and even aggregated keyword searches and tweets. These streams of electronic bits comprise, to a great degree, the public context of our time. Historians are the ideal reviewers of digital tools like Ngrams or Paper Machines, the critics who can tell where the data came from, which questions they can answer and which they cannot.

THE RESEARCH UNIVERSITY IS REBORN ... WITH AN ETHICAL SLANT

The methods for handling big data as a historic series of events are still new. We need tools for understanding the changing impact of ideas, individuals, and institutions over time. We need universities to educate students who can turn big data into *longue-durée* history, and use history to understand which data are applicable and which not. Were historians to return to the *longue durée*, rather than ignoring it or treating it purely second-hand, they would find themselves in the position of critics of the multiple kinds of data that we have outlined here. Climate data, biodiversity data, data about modern institutions and laws over the last millennia or previous five centuries, prison records, linguistic evidence of cultural change, grand-scale evidence of trade, migration, and displacement are all in the process of being compiled. What is desperately needed is a training capable of weaving them together into one inter-related fabric of time.

The era of fundamentalism about the past and its meaning is over – whether that fundamentalism preaches climate apocalypse, hunter-gatherer genes, or predestined capitalism for the few. Instead, it is time to look for leadership to the fields that have fastidiously analysed their data about the human experience and human institutions. We should invest in tools and forms of analysis that look critically at big data from multiple sources about the history and future of our institutions and societies. Our ability to creatively and knowledgeably shape a viable future in an era of multiple global challenges may depend upon it.

If these revolutions are to pass, historians themselves will have to change as well. They have a future to embrace on behalf of the public. They can confidently begin writing about the big picture, writing in a way transmissible to non-experts, talking about their data, and sharing their findings in a way that renders the power of their immense data at once understandable by an outsider. Their training should evolve to entertain conversations about what makes a good *longue durée* narrative, about how the archival skills of the micro-historian can be combined with the overarching suggestions offered by the macroscope. In the era of *longue-durée* tools, when experimenting across centuries becomes part of the toolkit of every graduate student, conversations about the appropriate audience and application of large-scale examinations of history may become part of the fabric of every History department. To reclaim their role as arbiters and synthesisers of knowledge about the past, historians will be indispensable to parse the data of anthropologists, evolutionary biologists, neuroscientists, historians of trade, historical economists, and historical geographers, weaving them into larger narratives that contextualise and make legible their claims and the foundations upon which they rest.

This challenge may have the effect of forcing historians to take a more active role in the many public institutions that govern the data about our past and future, not only government and activist data repositories but also libraries and archives, especially ones that run at cross-purposes with state-making projects where it would be convenient for certain political elites if the documentary evidence of particular ethnicities were erased altogether.[64] Societies in the grip of displacement are societies the least likely to have the resources to preserve their own histories. Someone must be responsible for the data that we – and future generations – use to understand what is happening in the world around us.

If historians are to take on the dual roles of arbiter of data for the public and investigator of forgotten stories, they will also need to take a more active part in preserving data and talking to the public about what is being preserved and what is not. Digitisation projects in a world dominated by anglophone conversations and nationalist archives raise issues of the representation of subalterns and developing nations, of minority languages and digital deficits. Where funding for digital documents is linked to nation building projects (as it is in many places), digital archives relating to women, minorities, and the poor risk not being digitised, or, where they are digitised, being underfunded or even unfunded. Just as books need correct temperature and humidity lest they decompose, so do digital documents require ongoing funding for their servers and maintenance for their bits. The strength of digital tools to promote *longue-durée* synthesis that includes perspectives other than that of the nation-state rests upon the ongoing creation and maintenance of inclusive archives.

Questions such as these draw deeply from the traditions of microhistory with its focus on how particular and vulnerable troves of testimony can illuminate the histories of slavery, capitalism, or domesticity. And, indeed, questions about how to preserve subaltern voices through the integration of micro-archives within the digitised record of the *longue durée* form a new and vitally important frontier of scholarship. That immense labour, and the critical thinking behind it, deserves to be recognised and rewarded through specially curated publications, grants, and prizes aimed at scholars who address the institutional work of the *longue-durée* micro-archive. This is another form of public work in the *longue durée*, one that aims less at public audiences and books with high sales or reading among bureaucrats than at the careful marshalling of documents, objects, stories, resources, and employment to create the micro-archival structure for macro-historical stories of genuine importance.

If historians – or any other historically minded scholars, from students of literature to sociologists – take up this challenge, they may find themselves in the avant garde of information design. They could collaborate with archivists, data scientists, economists, and climate scientists in the curating of larger and more synthetic databases for studying change over time. In the future, historians' expertise could be sought out in sectors beyond the university. Historians may become tool-builders and tool-reviewers as well as tool-consumers and tool-teachers. Indeed, these changes have the potential to revolutionise the life of some professional historians, as faculty provide data analysis for legislative committees, advise activist campaigns, or consult with Silicon Valley startups, and thereby regain the public role they traditionally occupied and deserve once more to regain. Changes such as these may in turn change both how and who we recruit as future historians, as time spent in other professional arenas or training in computer science will become a potential asset to the field.

In the future, we hope to look forward to digital projects that take advantage of computers' ability to analyse data at scale. We hope that modes of historiography will ponder the way these projects have or can make interventions in history produced by the single-scholar model of archival readings, synthesising current work and advancing the horizons of what an individual researcher will see. Above all, we hope that these problems of data from multiple sources – material, economic, demographic, political, and intellectual – can be overlaid against each other to produce unanticipated discoveries about change over time and the nature of the contemporary world in which we live.

The long-term perspective of the past can help those talking about the future to resist the kind of dogmatic thinking about past and future that we outlined in Chapter 3. In a world where creationists, environmentalists, and free-market theorists rarely argue against each other, we need experts who are willing to talk about our data in aggregate over the *longue durée*, to examine and compare the data around us, to weed out what is irrelevant and contrived, and to explain why and how they do so. History can serve as the arbiter here: it can put neo-liberalism, creation, and the environment on the same page; it can help undergraduates to negotiate their way through political and economic ideologies to a sensitivity of the culture of argumentation of many experts and the claims upon which their data rest.

Tools of critical historical thinking about where data come from, about multiple causality, and about bias will free us from the mythologies of natural laws propounded about market, state, and planetary fate in our time, stories that spell starvation and destruction for the masses. They will make clear that dogmatic thinking about the market or the climate that leads to the abandonment of our fellow human beings is a choice, and that other worlds are possible. And they will accomplish that by looking at the hard data of our planetary resources, their use, and the many alternatives displayed in the deep past and the various possible futures.

By focusing on perspectives such as these – and how they disrupt the institutions around us, and lead to better-informed citizens and more open government – universities can learn anew what it means to serve the public. Open-source, reusable tools, building upon existing resources, will encourage historians and indeed the public to look at events in their deep contexts, drawing out the most important narratives possible for a history of the present. Tools for synthesising information about change over time are of increasing importance in an era marked by a crisis about the future, when most institutions do their planning on cycles of less than five years. Yet the strength of big data and digital tools for analysis heralds a future where governments, activists, and the private sector all compete with their own models for understanding long-term prospects.

That demand for information about our past and future could create a new market for tools that synthesise enormous amounts of data about how climate and markets have changed and how governments and public experience have responded. In an era of expanding data, more of those tools for synthesis are surely coming. In the future, historians may step into new roles as data specialists, talking in public about other people's data, using their own scholarship to compare and contrast the methods of growth economists with the warnings of climate scientists.

There are many humanists and historians in the university who will baulk at an argument that data are indeed the future of the university. The decisions about whether to go long or short, whether to use received consensus or not, and how to use big data are as much ethical questions as methodological ones. Are we content, as historians, to leave the ostensible solutions to those crises in the hands of our colleagues in other academic departments? Or do we want to try to write good, honest history that would shake citizens, policymakers, and the powerful out of their complacency, history that will, in Simon Schama's words, 'keep people awake at night'?[65]

Conclusion:
the public future of the past

History's relationship with the public future lies in developing a *longue-durée* contextual background against which archival information, events, and sources can be interpreted. In the Introduction, we made the case that universities, founded to sustain and interrogate continuous traditions, had to face the challenges of that public future. In Chapter 1, we showed how much of our historical tradition was both public and future-oriented, not least the original *longue durée* proposed by Fernand Braudel. In Chapter 2, we argued that the *longue durée* was reviving after a period of comparative retreat among professional historians, but that its return was related to some of the most pressing global issues in public cultures around the world. In Chapter 3, we showed how that public future was served, albeit poorly and often at cross-purposes, by uncritical speculation about the future perils of climate, global governance, and inequality. We proposed that what was needed as a remedy was a turn towards a public future. And in Chapter 4, we illustrated some of the work for this collective scholarship about the future, based on a new and critical analysis of data about the past, that is already being done.

Responding to the call for a public future demands some rethinking the way we look at the past. We have already talked about the power of big data to illuminate the shadows of history, to test received wisdom and to interrogate reigning theories about the past. But answering the call for a public future also means writing and talking about the past and the future *in public*, in such a way that ideas can be easily shared. We believe that this dedication to the public heralds three new trends in the writing of history: first, a need for new narratives capable of being read, understood, and engaged by non-experts; second, an emphasis on visualisation and digital tools; and third, a fusion between the big and the small, the 'micro' and the 'macro', that harnesses the best of archival work on the one hand and big-picture work about issues of common concern on the other.

If long-term historical thinking is to fulfil the promise we have proposed for it here, then we will need a rubric for thinking big with adequate skill and historical finesse. What constitutes a critical eye for looking at long-term stories? What characteristics unite the models that we choose? How would a classroom training young minds to think far back and far forward in time operate? We sum up this book by looking back over the arguments we have drawn together, and by pulling out major ways of thinking about the long-term future. That task, we believe, requires the services of scholars trained in looking at the past, who can explain where things came from, who can examine the precise evidence of the Short Past and the broader picture of big data and the *longue durée,* and who are dedicated to serve the public through responsible thinking about the nexus of past, present, and future. These methods may offer a recipe for change in the university and for the sciences of prediction and future response at large.

In a moment of expanding inequality, amid crises of global governance, and under the impact of anthropogenic climate change, even a minimal understanding of the conditions shaping our lives demands a scaling-up of our inquiries. As the *longue durée* returns, in a new guise with new goals, it still demands a response to the most basic issues of historical methodology – of what problems we select, how we choose the boundaries of our topic, and what tools we put to solving our questions. The seeds of a new conversation about the future of the past and the big picture are already planted, indeed they represent the reasons why Big History, Deep History, and the Anthropocene are on the rise already. In other subfields, a new synthesis has also begun, albeit rarely explicitly critical of data, visualisation-oriented, or directed to the public, activists, or policy.

An era defined by a crisis of short-termism may be a particularly good time to start rethinking attitudes towards the past. Many histories have been written with the express purpose of offering a window into the future, and some – especially long-term histories of capitalism and the environment – are very clear about what they offer. Reflecting on the power of reading a history book that shows how modern game-theory came out of the Cold War industrial complex, the University of California historian Sanford Jacoby enthuses, 'We should be the ones taking the lead on developing cross-disciplinary, big-think courses'. Jacoby teaches at a business school, where, he writes, 'The students, it is said, fail to get "the big picture" and cannot escape the conceptual fetters of the present moment. Historians have a lot to offer here.'[1] To respond to such challenges, those who deal in knowledge of the past should be unafraid of generating and circulating digestible narratives, condensing new research about political, economic, and environmental history for a public audience.

The public needs stories about how we came to be at the brink of an ecological crisis and a crisis of inequality. The moral stakes of *longue-durée* subjects – including the reorientation of our economy to cope with global warming and the integration of subaltern experience into policy – mandate that historians choose as large an audience as possible for all of the human experiences about which they write – including (but certainly not limited to) problems of the environment, governance, democracy, and capitalism. In the university, much may need to change to make room for forms of inquiry that concentrate on public knowledge of our mutual future. Journals that exist behind pay-walls, accessible only to those with access to major public or university libraries, need to be supplemented by open-access sources available to wider global publics.[2] We also need informative visualisations of our research and to put them in public, and peer-review the research behind them quickly and efficiently with the agenda of forming a new, crucial, and politically informed synthesis.

Micro-history and macro-history – short-term analysis and the long-term overview – should work together to produce a more intense, sensitive, and ethical synthesis of data. Critical history is capable of addressing both the macro and the micro, of talking about how small and repressed experiences add up to the overturning of nations and empires. As Lynn Hunt rightly notes, 'A global, mega-long-term history is not the only story to be told', but such long-term histories do need to be articulated with the fruits of more precise and local histories and vice versa: 'The scale of the study depends on the question to be answered.'[3] It is not that micro-histories or short-term studies of any sort are not critical – far from it. In pointing to the challenge that history can offer to the mythologies of neo-liberal economics and climate catastrophism, much of our evidence here is gathered from the work of historians who worked hard in the archives, with deeply controversial questions driving their inquiries. But the rule in the training of historians, at least since the 1970s, has been one that often discouraged thinking about the big picture in favour of the assiduous concentration on sources from particular archives approached with particular procedures of critical reading.

With regard to the marriage of micro-historical and macro-historical into a synthetic understanding of our past, the field of anthropology is often ahead of history. Consider the *longue-durée* histories of Southeast Asia by James C. Scott into the deep history of the highland mountains on the fringe of Chinese Empire he calls Zomia. Zomia, he finds, is defined by the flight of people from oppressive political and economic regimes, whence they recoil into a subsistence-like existence, a trade in wild spices and roots rather than cultivated gardens, egalitarian political forms rather than hierarchical ones, a prophetic culture rather than received religion, and timeless stories rather than the recitation of history. Again, a series of micro-histories of hill-people, assembled across the centuries, becomes a powerful macro-story with which to destabilise received accounts of the inevitability of empire, centralisation, capitalism, or hierarchy.[4]

Anthropology is probably able to execute such long-term analysis that wholly overturns received accounts of the institutions that necessarily do or should typify modernity, largely because it is not as exercised by the micro–macro distinctions as history. The micro is allowed to become the 'exceptional typical' that both proves the rule and exemplifies how a dominant superstructure is overturned.[5] No scholar should argue for eliminating this important micro-work, the recovery of the subaltern and the patient sifting of the archives, from the work of history. Indeed, in his daring macro-histories, Scott has lately advised that scholars should revise their studies of nations and peoples into studies of particular families and their interactions over time. In the same way, historians can salvage the search for crucial pivots, turning-points, and clues, by which outstanding normal experience can illuminate the whole. And then history must illuminate the whole again.

The revived *longue durée* that we hope for is one that will continue micro-history's work of destabilising modernisation narratives,

Whig history, and other forms of teleological thinking. But micro-history that fails to reconnect to larger narratives, and to state frankly what it hopes to overturn and what to uphold, may court antiquarianism. What we hope for is a kind of history with a continuing role for micro-historical, archival work embedded within a larger macro-story woven from a broad range of sources. In this way, the often shocking and informative events drawn from the lives of actual persons must continue to be a source of circumspection and critical analysis for historians, even as they take their arguments wider. It is not necessary to relate every link in the chain of a *longue-durée* narrative in micro-historical detail: a serial history, of richly recovered moments cast within a larger framework, may be adequate to show continuities across time along with the specificities of particular instances.[6]

A *longue-durée* introduction that spans the disciplines and makes the author's targets clear may amplify the message of short-*durée* archival research. But without that *longue-durée* frame, the micro-history may be lost in the debate altogether. Together, micro-historical work in archives and macro-historical frameworks can offer a new horizon for historical researchers who want to hone their talents of judging the flow of events and institutions across centuries and around the globe. A long-term story that reduces a great deal of information into a crystalline packet, writes Paul Carter, has the effect of rendering large numbers of facts compact, transportable, and shareable, 'like a cake of portable soup'.[7] In any moment of political divergence, historical synthesis can help to form consensus where consensus has been lost. At a moment when the public again needs long-term stories, these modes of analysis become important in how we tell stories, how analysts design tools, and how universities offer historical training to future scholars and citizens.

Not all fields have the same problem manufacturing condensed pictures of their research for public consumption. The discipline of economics specialised in easily transmissible charts and graphs from the 1930s, when new methods of visualisation were pioneered by left-wing economists like Rex Tugwell of the University of Chicago with the agenda of gathering public support for new, government-directed programmes of infrastructure and employment. Those charts and summaries circulated and were republished in newspapers, magazines, and policy papers, being more concise and reproducible than their equivalent twenty-page essay in the hands of text-based scholars such as historians. To be sure, their policies often flattered entrenched interests and promised little disruption; they bought off potential admirers with promises of unlimited growth.[8] But the environmentalists, with all their data, never got as far as making promises or describing next steps. They rarely condensed their theories into legible charts and graphics that could circulate widely beyond academic circles.

In the world of the digital university, tools are circulating that can consolidate and condense so much writing into discrete visualisations, which allow historians to imitate economists in sharing one-screen visual versions of their arguments: 'shock and awe visualisations', as their critics call them. Already Twitter and blogs demonstrate how historians are investigating alternative routes in publishing, ones that are easy to pass around, good at going viral, and powerfully infectious of discourse. We were all astonished to see the social network maps of the letters of Smith, Voltaire, and Franklin lit up in orange across the black map of Europe when Stanford released its first Mapping the Republic of Letters Project. But the real significance of that map may be that it was among the first data-driven digital history projects to circulate to a wider public, for example in the pages of the *New York Times*.[9] These realities should drive scholars, particularly humanists and historians, to be interested in teaching, publishing, and innovating the modelling change over time with various word-count, quantitative, topic-modelling, and other timeline-generating visualisations.

Micro-historians have been working for a long time to challenge claims that capitalism naturally diminishes inequality. Indeed, centuries of data give an enormous pile of evidence to the contrary – that rather than leading to more equality, capitalism tends to exacerbate divides of class, even of race and gender. Despite the enormous number of books that have been written on the subject of perpetuated inequalities of capitalism, the public has rarely paid attention to these arguments. The convenient visualisations of economists, suggesting that capitalism means decreasing unemployment and rising equality, have been easier to circulate. Almost the only historical data that have been able to challenge that easy consensus have been Piketty's *Capital in the Twenty-First Century* – historical data that are framed in terms of convenient visualisations of massive data, aggregated over the long term, as discussed in Chapter 3.

There is an older tradition that looks to history as the guide of public conversations about the future. Indeed, the popularity of reenactment, 'reality' history TV, computer games with historical settings, and historical series suggests something of the continuing claims of history on the public imagination.[10] More than that, a public need to make sense of our common past, recent and deep alike, has driven for thirty years the production of historically framed arguments by economists and climate scientists struggling to make sense of prosperity, pollution, and human nature itself. Whether or not professional historians are willing to join these conversations, public discourse cannot do without a long-term perspective on the past and the future. Indeed, for reasons of encouraging this kind of engagement, higher education and research councils in Australia, Europe, and the United Kingdom have mandated public engagement, 'impact', and 'relevance' as criteria for evaluating university performance.[11] While some academics shudder at this seeming intrusion into how they choose their audiences and subjects, others see a profound opportunity for service.

The tools of looking at the past in the service of the future offer an important role for the university as arbiter of falsity, myth, and noise in an age overwhelmed by big data, where future risk takes the form of problems of unprecedented scale like climate change and transnational governance. Looking to the micro-past and macro-past together offers a useful model for understanding the stakes and implications of changes that range from institutional forces shaped over the last decade to climatic forces shaped over the millennia of evolution. As the historian of public policy Pamela Cox has noted, historians 'need to be prepared to move beyond the confines of our "period" when necessary and to swap our fine brushes for broader ones so as to paint new "grand narratives" of social change that are not crudely determinist but are critical, structural and sceptical'.[12]

We have argued for History as a critical human science with a public mission. History is not unique in having a vocation to enlighten and reform, at least if it is compared with the other disciplines – sociology, anthropology, political science – usually collected under the umbrella of the social sciences rather than juxtaposed with sibling disciplines in the humanities, such as philology or musicology. As Craig Calhoun, former head of the American Social Science Research Council and Director of the London School of Economics, has pointed out, 'Public engagement was a strong feature of the social sciences from their birth'. And yet, he goes on to note, the public relevance of the social sciences declined with specialisation and their retreat into the academy. His diagnosis parallels ours, even though he does not treat History specifically among the human sciences. A lost sense of public purpose; a weakening grasp on the big picture; exploding scholarly productivity (often under externally imposed regimes of assessment and 'impact'); a proliferation of 'histories' rather than 'history'; greater prestige for novelty and discovery rather than synthesis and theory: all these are familiar features of the human sciences in the late twentieth and early twenty-first centuries.[13] History has shared many of the same problems of successful professionalisation. The challenge now is to hold on to the palpable benefits of professionalism while also recovering connections with a broader public mission that remains critical rather than merely affirmatory.

Looking to the past to shape the future offers an important call to historians, historical sociologists, historical geographers, and information scientists in particular. It also provides a roadmap for thinking prospectively to all of those institutions – government, finance, insurance, informal, self-organised, citizen-scientific, and other – that we call upon to guide us as we seek the road to better futures. There are traditions available to those who seek that road, and all of them have a track record. The past, we believe, is the best indicator of future behaviour for all of them. 'Surely history need not simply be condemned to the study of well-walled gardens', wrote Fernand Braudel: 'If it is will it not fail in its present tasks, of responding to the agonizing problems of the hour and of keeping in touch with the human sciences, which are at once so young and so imperialistic? Can there be any humanism at the present time ... without an ambitious history, conscious of its duties and its great powers?'[14] His questions are as timely, as pressing now as when Braudel first posed them, in 1946.

The public future of the past remains in the hands of historians, 'if we are willing to look out of our study windows and to think of history, not as the property of a small guild of professional colleagues, but as the rightful heritage of millions'.[15] The words are those of the American historian J. Franklin Jameson, first delivered in December 1912 but, like Braudel's, they remain urgently relevant today. Over the past century, the historical profession has undertaken the series of turns we anatomised earlier in this book: social, cultural, gendered, imperial, postcolonial, global, and transnational among them. Armed by now with critical transnational and transtemporal perspectives, historians can be guardians against parochial perspectives and endemic short-termism. Once called upon to offer their advice on political development and land-reform, the creation of the welfare state and post-conflict settlement, historians, along with other humanists, effectively ceded the public arena, nationally as well as globally, to the economists and occasionally lawyers and political scientists. (When was the last time a historian was seconded to Downing Street or the White House from their academic post, let alone consulted for the World Bank or advised the UN Secretary-General?) It may be little wonder, then, that we have a crisis of global governance, that we are all at the mercy of unregulated financial markets, and that anthropogenic climate change threatens our political stability and the survival of species. To put these challenges in perspective, and to combat the short-termism of our time, we urgently need the wide-angle, long-range views only historians can provide.

Historians of the world, unite! There is a world to win – before it's too late.

Notes

INTRODUCTION: THE BONFIRE OF THE HUMANITIES?

1 Alfred Rappaport, *Saving Capitalism from Short-termism: How to Build Long-term Value and Take Back our Financial Future* (New York, 2011); Dominic Barton and Mark Wiseman, 'Focusing Capital on the Long Term', *Harvard Business Review* 92, 1–2 (January–February 2014), 44–51.

2 Stewart Brand, *The Clock of the Long Now: Time and Responsibility* (New York, 1999), 3: http://longnow.org/.

3 Pascal Lamy *et al.*, *Now for the Long Term: The Report of the Oxford Martin Commission for Future Generations* (Oxford, 2013), 6, 9.

4 Francis Fukuyama, *The End of History and the Last Man* (New York, 2006); Thomas L. Friedman, *Hot, Flat, and Crowded: Why We Need a Green Revolution – And How it Can Renew America* (New York, 2008).

5 The inspiration for these popularisations comes from works such as Steven D. Levitt and Stephen J. Dubner, *Freakonomics: A Rogue Economist Explores the Hidden Side of Everything* (New York, 2005); Gregory Clark, *A Farewell to Alms: A Brief Economic History of the World* (Princeton, NJ, 2007); and Francis Fukuyama, *The Origins of Political Order: From Prehuman Times to the French Revolution* (New York, 2011).

6 'The World's Oldest Companies', *The Economist* (16 December 2004): www.economist.com/node/3490684.

7 Stefan Collini, *What Are Universities For?* (London, 2012); Andrew McGettigan, *The Great University Gamble: Money, Markets and the Future of Higher Education* (London, 2013).

8 Michael Spence, 'How Best to Measure the Value of Research', *The Chronicle of Higher Education* (8 August 2013): http://chronicle.com/blogs/worldwise/how-best-to-measure-the-value-of-research/32765.

9 Rens Bod, *A New History of the Humanities: The Search for Principles and Patterns from Antiquity to the Present* (Oxford, 2013).

10 Lynn Hunt, *Writing History in the Global Era* (New York, 2014), 1.

11 Important recent defences of the humanities from Britain and the United States include Louis Menand, *The Marketplace of Ideas* (New York, 2010); Martha Nussbaum, *Not for Profit: Why Democracy Needs the Humanities* (Princeton, NJ, 2010); Jonathan Bate (ed.), *The Public Value of the Humanities* (London, 2011); Helen Small, *The Value of the Humanities* (Oxford, 2013).

12 Daniel Lord Smail, 'Introduction: History and the Telescoping of Time: A Disciplinary Forum', *French Historical Studies* 34 (2011), 1, 2.

13 David Christian, 'The Longest Durée: A History of the Last 15 Billion Years', *Australian Historical Association Bulletin,* 59–60 (August–November 1989), 27–36; Christian, 'Big History: The Longest "Durée"', *Österreichische Zeitschrift für Geschichtswissenschaften* 20 (2009), 91–106; Tom Griffiths, 'Travelling in Deep Time: *La Longue Durée* in Australian History', *Australian Humanities Review* (June 2000): www.australian humanitiesreview.org/archive/Issue-June-2000/griffiths4.html.

14 David Armitage and Jo Guldi, 'Le Retour de la longue durée. Une perspective anglo-saxonne', *Annales. Histoire, Sciences sociales,* 70 (2015). More generally, see Barbara Weinstein, 'History Without a Cause? Grand Narratives, World History, and the Postcolonial Dilemma', *International Review of Social History* 50 (2005), 71–93; Penelope Corfield, 'The Big Picture's Past, Present and Future', *The Times Higher* (27 July 2007), 14; Donald A. Yerxa, 'Introduction: History on a Large Scale', in Yerxa (ed.), *World History and the History of the West: Historians in Conversation* (Columbia, SC, 2009), 1–12; David Christian, 'The Return of Universal History', *History and Theory* 49 (2010), 6–27; David Sebouh Aslanian *et al.*, 'How Size Matters: The Question of Scale in History', *American Historical Review* 118 (2013), 1431–72.

15 Richard Drayton, 'Imperial History and the Human Future', *History Workshop Journal,* 74 (2012), 167.

16 Fernand Braudel, 'Histoire et Sciences sociales. La longue durée', *Annales. Histoire, Sciences sociales* 13 (1958), 725–53; trans. as Braudel, 'History and the Social Sciences', in Braudel, *On History* (trans.) Sarah Matthews (Chicago, 1982), 25–54.

17 Pierre Bourdieu, 'The Field of Cultural Production, or: The Economic World Reversed', in Bourdieu, *The Field of Cultural Production: Essays on Art and Literature* (ed. and introd.) Randal Johnson (New York, 1993), 60.

CHAPTER I GOING FORWARD BY LOOKING BACK:
THE RISE OF THE *LONGUE DURÉE*

1 Michel de Certeau, *The Writing of History* (trans.) Tom Conley (New York, 1988).

2 Winston Churchill, toast to the Royal College of Physicians (2 March 1944): 'Prime Minister Among the Physicians', *The Lancet* 243 (11 March 1944), 344; Peter Clarke, *Mr Churchill's Profession: Statesman, Orator, Writer* (London, 2012).

3 For example, Richard L. Bushman, *The Refinement of America: Persons, Houses, Cities* (New York, 1993); Norbert Elias, *The Civilizing Process:*

Sociogenetic and Psychogenetic Investigations (trans.) Edmund Jephcott, rev. edn (Oxford, 2000).

4 Quentin Skinner, 'Meaning and Understanding in the History of Ideas', *History and Theory* 8 (1969), 3–53.

5 Wilhelm Windelband, 'Rectorial Address, Strasbourg, 1894' (trans.) Guy Oakes, *History and Theory* 19 (1980), 169–85.

6 David Armitage, 'What's the Big Idea? Intellectual History and the *Longue Durée*', *History of European Ideas* 38 (2012), 493–507.

7 Fernand Braudel, 'History and the Social Sciences: The *Longue Durée*' (1958), in Braudel, *On History* (trans.) Sarah Matthews (Chicago, 1982), 47.

8 William H. Sewell, Jr, *Logics of History: Social Theory and Social Transformation* (Chicago, 2005).

9 Fernand Braudel, 'Histoire et Sciences sociales. La longue durée', *Annales. Histoire, Sciences sociales* 13 (1958), 725–53.

10 Fernand Braudel, 'Préface' (1946), in *La Méditerranée et le Monde méditerranéen à l'époque de Philippe II* (Paris, 1949), xiii.

11 A charge immediately rejected by Witold Kula, 'Histoire et économie. Le longue durée', *Annales. Histoire, Sciences sociales* 15 (1960), 294–313.

12 Braudel, 'Histoire et Sciences sociales', 735, 751.

13 See, for example, Eugène Garsonnet, *Histoire des locations perpétuelles et des baux à longue durée* (Paris, 1878); Victor Lemaitre, *Considérations sur la paralysie générale de longue durée* (Paris, 1879); Gaston Imbert, *Des mouvements de longue durée Kondratieff*, 3 vols. (Aix-en-Provence, 1956).

14 Peter Burke, *The French Historical Revolution: The Annales School, 1929–89* (Oxford, 1990), 33; Paule Braudel, 'Braudel en captivité', in Paul Carmignani (ed.), *Autour de F. Braudel* (Perpignan, 2001), 13–25; Peter Schöttler, 'Fernand Braudel als Kriegsgefangener in Deutschland', in Fernand Braudel, *Geschichte als Schlüssel zur Welt. Vorlesungen in Deutscher Kriegsgefangenschaft 1941* (ed.) Peter Schöttler (Stuttgart, 2013), 187–211. Braudel's lectures in the camps have been reconstructed as 'L'Histoire, mesure du monde' (1941–4), in Fernand Braudel, *Les ambitions de l'Histoire* (ed.) Roselyne de Ayala and Paule Braudel (Paris, 1997), 13–83.

15 Giuliana Gemelli, *Fernand Braudel e l'Europa universale* (Venice, 1990), 246–300; Maurice Aymard, 'La longue durée aujourd'hui. Bilan d'un demi-siècle (1958–2008)', in Diogo Ramada Curto, Eric R. Dursteller, Julius Kirshner, and Francesca Trivellato (eds.), *From Florence to the Mediterranean and Beyond: Essays in Honour of Anthony Molho*, 2 vols. (Florence, 2009), II, 559–60 (quoted).

16 Fernand Braudel, 'Gaston Berger, 1896–1960', *Annales. Histoire, Sciences sociales* 16 (1961), 210–11; Gaston Berger, *Phénoménologie du temps et prospective* (Paris, 1964); Gemelli, *Fernand Braudel e l'Europa universale*,

301–62; Jenny Andersson, 'The Great Future Debate and the Struggle for the World', *American Historical Review* 117 (2012), 1417–18.

17 Cicero, *De Oratore*, 11.36: 'Historia vero testis temporum, lux veritatis, vita memoriae, magistra vitae, nuntia vetustatis, qua voce alia nisi oratoris immortalitati commendatur?' ('By what voice other than the orator's is history – the witness of past times, the light of truth, the life of memory, the guide to life, the herald of antiquity – entrusted to immortality?')

18 John Burrow, *A History of Histories: Epics, Chronicles, Romances and Inquiries from Herodotus and Thucydides to the Twentieth Century* (London, 2007), 163–4.

19 Burrow, *A History of Histories*, 366, 426; Deborah Wormell, *Sir John Seeley and the Uses of History* (Cambridge, 1980), ch. 4, 'School of Statesmanship'.

20 Alfred Thayer Mahan, *The Influence of Sea Power Upon History, 1660–1783* (Boston, 1890); Mark Russell Shulman, 'The Influence of Mahan upon Sea Power', *Reviews in American History* 19 (1991), 522–7.

21 John Keegan, *The Face of Battle* (London, 1976); Peter Paret, Gordon A. Craig, and Felix Gilbert (eds.), *Makers of Modern Strategy: From Machiavelli to the Nuclear Age* (Princeton, NJ, 1986); John Keegan, *A History of Warfare* (New York, 1993); Allan D. English (ed.), *The Changing Face of War: Learning from History* (Montreal, 1998); Azar Gat, *A History of Military Thought: From the Enlightenment to the Cold War* (Oxford, 2001); Jo Guldi, 'The Uses of Planning and the Decay of Strategy', *Contemporary Security Policy* 27 (2006), 209–36; Williamson Murray, *War, Strategy, and Military Effectiveness* (Cambridge, 2011); Hew Strachan, *The Direction of War: Contemporary Strategy in Historical Perspective* (Cambridge, 2013).

22 Williamson Murray and Richard Hart Sinnreich (eds.), *The Past as Prologue: The Importance of History to the Military Profession* (Cambridge, 2006).

23 Louis Geoffroy, *Napoléon apocryphe, 1812–1832: histoire de la conquête du monde & de la monarchie universelle* (Paris, 1836); Catherine Gallagher, 'What Would Napoleon Do? Historical, Fictional, and Counterfactual Characters', *New Literary History* 42 (2011), 323–5.

24 Sidney and Beatrice Webb, *English Local Government*, 11 vols. (London, 1906–29).

25 Gertrude Himmelfarb, 'The Intellectual in Politics: The Case of the Webbs', *Journal of Contemporary History* 6 (1971), 3.

26 Adam Kuper, 'The Rise and Fall of Maine's Patriarchal Society', in Alan Diamond (ed.), *The Victorian Achievement of Sir Henry Maine* (Cambridge, 1991), 100–10; C. Hill, 'Sidney Webb and the Common Good: 1887–1889', *History of Political Thought* 14 (1993), 591–622.

27 Sidney Webb, 'The Basis of Socialism: Historic', in George Bernard Shaw (ed.), *Fabian Essays in Socialism* (1889) (London, 1948), 29, 32, 46–7.

28 Sidney Webb, *The London Programme* (London, 1891); Asa Briggs, *Victorian Cities* (London, 1963), 350–2.

29 John Broich, *London: Water and the Making of the Modern City* (Pittsburgh, 2013).

30 R. H. Tawney, *The Agrarian Problem in the Sixteenth Century* (London, 1912).

31 R. H. Tawney, *A Memorandum on Agriculture and Industry in China* (Honolulu, 1929); Tawney, *Land and Labour in China* (London, 1932); Lawrence Goldman, *The Life of R. H. Tawney: Socialism and History* (London, 2013), 147.

32 E. J. Hobsbawm, *Labouring Men: Studies in the History of Labour* (London, 1965); Hobsbawm, *Primitive Rebels: Studies in Archaic Forms of Social Movement in the 19th and 20th Centuries* (London, 1965); Hobsbawm, *The Age of Revolution: Europe 1789–1848* (London, 1962).

33 E. J. Hobsbawm, 'The Social Function of the Past: Some Questions', *Past & Present* 55 (1972), 3–17; Hobsbawm, *On History* (New York, 1997); Hobsbawm, *On the Edge of the New Century* (London, 2000); Hobsbawm, *On Empire: America, War, and Global Supremacy* (London, 2008); Gregory Elliott, *Hobsbawm: History and Politics* (London, 2010).

34 Charles Beard, *American Government and Politics* (New York, 1910); Charles Beard and Mary Beard, *The Rise of American Civilization* (New York, 1928); Merle Curti, *The American Peace Crusade, 1815–1860* (Durham, NC, 1929); Curti, *Peace or War: The American Struggle* (New York, 1936).

35 J. L. Hammond and Barbara Hammond, *The Village Labourer, 1760–1832: A Study in the Government of England before the Reform Bill* (London, 1911); Karl Polanyi, *The Great Transformation* (New York, 1944); W. G. Hoskins, *The Making of the English Landscape* (London, 1955); M. W. Beresford, *History on the Ground: Six Studies in Maps and Landscapes* (London, 1957).

36 Jawaharlal Nehru, *Glimpses of World History* (Kitabistan, 1934); Vinayak Domodar Savarkar, *Six Glorious Epochs of Indian History* (Delhi, 1963); C. L. R. James, *State Capitalism and World Revolution* (Chicago, 1986); James, *The Future in the Present* (London, 1977).

37 Hannah Arendt, *The Human Condition* (Chicago, 1958); Arendt, *The Origins of Totalitarianism* (New York, 1958); Arendt, *Between Past and Future: Six Exercises in Political Thought* (New York, 1961).

38 Lewis Mumford, *The Story of Utopias* (New York, 1922); Mumford, *Technics and Civilization* (New York, 1934); Mumford, *The Culture of*

Cities (New York, 1938); Thomas P. Hughes, *Lewis Mumford: Public Intellectual* (Oxford, 1990).

39 Charles Beard, *American Government and Politics* (New York, 1910, and later edns); Arthur Schlesinger, Sr, *Political and Social History of the United States, 1829–1925* (New York, 1925, and later edns).

40 For example, Lewis Mumford, 'The Intolerable City: Must It Keep on Growing?', *Harper's Magazine* 152 (1926), 283–93; Mumford, 'Magnified Impotence', *New Republic* 49 (22 December 1926), 138–40; Mumford, 'The Sky Line: Bigger Slums or Better City?', *The New Yorker* 26 (24 June 1950), 78–84.

41 William Appleman Williams, *The Tragedy of American Diplomacy* (New York, 1962); Kevin Mattson, *Intellectuals in Action: The Origins of the New Left and Radical Liberalism, 1945–1970* (University Park, PA, 2002), 147–51, 159.

42 John Boyd Orr, *A Short History of British Agriculture* (London, 1922). The book remained relatively unknown, but Orr's historically derived view of how institutions could revolutionise agriculture was put into practice on a global scale over the coming decades by the UN organs that he helped to found.

43 David Landes, *The Unbound Prometheus: Technological Change and Industrial Development in Western Europe from 1750 to the Present* (London, 1969); William J. Ashworth, 'The British Industrial Revolution and the Ideological Revolution: Science, Neoliberalism and History', *History of Science* (2014): doi: 10.1177/0073275314529860.

44 Elias H. Tuma, *Twenty-Six Centuries of Agrarian Reform: A Comparative Analysis* (Berkeley, 1965); Russell King, *Land Reform: A World Survey* (London, 1977).

45 Alfred N. Chandler, *Land Title Origins: A Tale of Force and Fraud* (New York, 1945).

46 George Raymond Geiger, *The Theory of the Land Question* (New York, 1936); Paolo Grossi, *An Alternative to Private Property: Collective Property in the Juridical Consciousness of the Nineteenth Century* (trans.) Lydia G. Cochrane (Chicago, 1981).

47 Aaron M. Sakolski, *Land Tenure and Land Taxation in America* (New York, 1957), 13; compare Eric Nelson, *The Hebrew Republic: Jewish Sources and the Transformation of European Political Thought* (Cambridge, MA, 2010), 57–87.

48 Charles Dupin, *The Commercial Power of Great Britain* (1824) (Eng. trans.), 2 vols. (London, 1825).

49 See, for example, Paul R. Ehrlich, *The Population Bomb* (New York, 1968); Erich Fromm, *The Revolution of Hope: Toward a Humanized Technology* (New York, 1968); R. Buckminster Fuller, *Utopia or Oblivion: The Prospects for Humanity* (London, 1969); Alvin Toffler, *Future*

Shock (New York, 1970); Norman Borlaug, *Mankind and Civilization at Another Crossroad* (Madison, WI, 1971); Herman Kahn and B. Bruce-Briggs, *Things to Come: Thinking about the Seventies and Eighties* (New York, 1972); George Leonard, *The Transformation: A Guide to the Inevitable Changes in Humankind* (New York, 1972); Donella Meadows *et al.*, *The Limits to Growth: A Report for the Club of Rome's Project on the Predicament of Mankind* (New York, 1972); Adrian Berry, *The Next Ten Thousand Years: A Vision of Man's Future in the Universe* (New York, 1974); Mihajlo Mesarović and Eduard Pestel, *Mankind at the Turning Point: The Second Report to the Club of Rome* (New York, 1974); Herman Kahn, William Brown, and Leon Martel, *The Next 200 Years: A Scenario for America and the World* (New York, 1976); Wayne I. Boucher (ed.), *The Study of the Future: An Agenda for Research* (Washington, DC, 1977); Ervin László *et al.*, *Goals for Mankind: A Report to the Club of Rome on the New Horizons of Global Community* (New York, 1977).

50 Herman Kahn, William Brown, and Leon Martel, *The Next 200 Years: A Scenario for America and the World* (New York, 1976); Paul Dragoş Aligică, *Prophecies of Doom and Scenarios of Progress: Herman Kahn, Julian Simon, and the Prospective Imagination* (New York, 2007); Andersson, 'The Great Future Debate and the Struggle for the World', 1416.

51 Mike Hulme, 'Reducing the Future to Climate: A Story of Climate Determinism and Reductionism', *Osiris* 26 (2011), 256.

52 Libby Robin, 'Histories for Changing Times: Entering the Anthropocene?', *Australian Historical Studies* 44 (2013), 333.

53 Bill Vitek and Wes Jackson (eds.), *The Virtues of Ignorance: Complexity, Sustainability, and the Limits of Knowledge* (Lexington, KY, 2008); Wes Jackson, *Consulting the Genius of the Place: An Ecological Approach to a New Agriculture* (Berkeley, 2010).

54 Niall Ferguson (ed.), *Virtual History: Alternatives and Counterfactuals* (London, 1997); Richard Evans, *Altered Pasts: Counterfactuals in History* (London, 2014).

55 Humberto Llavador, John E. Roemer, and Joaquim Silvestre, 'A Dynamic Analysis of Human Welfare in a Warming Planet', *Journal of Public Economics* 95 (2011), 1607–20; Llavador, Roemer, and Silvestre, *Sustainability for a Warming Planet* (Cambridge, MA, 2015).

56 Ted Steinberg, 'Can Capitalism Save the Planet? On the Origins of Green Liberalism', *Radical History Review* 107 (2010), 7–24; Emma Rothschild, Paul Warde, and Alison Frank, 'Forum: The Idea of Sustainability', *Modern Intellectual History* 8 (2011), 147–212; Joshua J. Yates, 'Abundance on Trial: The Cultural Significance of "Sustainability"', *The Hedgehog Review* 14 (2012), 8–25.

57 World Commission on Environment and Development, *Our Common Future* (New York, 1987); Paul B. Thompson, *The Agrarian Vision: Sustainability and Environmental Ethics* (Lexington, KY, 2010), 197–200.

58 Mumford, *The Story of Utopias*; Gregory Claeys, *Searching for Utopia: The History of an Idea* (London, 2011).

59 Wes Jackson, *New Roots for Agriculture* (San Francisco, 1980).

60 Martin Mulligan and Stuart Hill, *Ecological Pioneers: A Social History of Australian Ecological Thought and Action* (Cambridge, 2001), 195–200.

61 L. C. Jain and Karen Coelho, *In the Wake of Freedom: India's Tryst with Cooperatives* (New Delhi, 1996); John Curl, 'The Cooperative Movement in Century 21', *Affinities: A Journal of Radical Theory, Culture, and Action* 4 (2010), 12–29; John Restakis, *Humanizing the Economy: Co-operatives in the Age of Capital* (Philadelphia, 2010); John Curl, *For All the People* (Oakland, CA, 2012); John F. Wilson, Anthony Webster, and Rachael Vorberg-Rugh, *Building Co-operation: A Business History of the Co-operative Group, 1863–2013* (Oxford, 2013); Jessica Gordon Nembhard, *Collective Courage: A History of African American Cooperative Economic Thought and Practice* (University Park, PA, 2014).

62 William H. McNeill, 'Organizing Concepts for World History', *World History Bulletin* 4 (1986–7), 1–4; Peter N. Stearns, 'Periodization in World History Teaching: Identifying the Big Changes', *The History Teacher* 20 (1987), 561–80.

63 William A. Green, 'Periodization in European and World History', *Journal of World History* 3 (1992), 13–53; Jerry H. Bentley, 'Cross-Cultural Interaction and Periodization in World History', *American Historical Review* 101 (1996), 749–70.

64 Jürgen Osterhammel, *The Transformation of the World: A Global History of the Nineteenth Century* (Princeton, NJ, 2014), 48. See also Wolfgang Reinhard, 'The Idea of Early Modern History', in Michael Bentley (ed.), *Companion to Historiography* (London, 1997), 290; Penelope Corfield, *Time and the Shape of History* (New Haven, 2007), 134–8.

65 Manuel De Landa, *A Thousand Years of Nonlinear History* (New York, 1997).

CHAPTER 2 THE SHORT PAST: OR, THE RETREAT
OF THE *LONGUE DURÉE*

1 E. J. Hobsbawm, *Primitive Rebels: Studies in Archaic Forms of Social Movement in the 19th and 20th Centuries* (Manchester, 1959); Hobsbawm, *The Age of Revolution, 1789–1848* (London, 1962); Hobsbawm, *Labouring Men: Studies in the History of Labour* (London, 1964); Hobsbawm, *Industry and Empire: The Making of Modern English Society, 1750 to the Present Day* (London, 1968); Hobsbawm, *Bandits* (New York, 1969). On 1968, see Ronald Fraser, *1968: A Student Generation in Revolt* (New York, 1988); Michael Seidman, *The Imaginary Revolution: Parisian*

Students and Workers in 1968 (New York, 2004); Rainer Horn, *The Spirit of '68: Rebellion in Western Europe and North America, 1956–1976* (Oxford, 2007); Martin Klimke, *The Other Alliance: Student Protest in West Germany and the United States in the Global Sixties* (Princeton, NJ, 2011).

2 Geoff Eley, *A Crooked Line: From Cultural History to the History of Society* (Ann Arbor, MI, 2005), ix.

3 Geoff Eley, 'The German Navy League in German Politics, 1898–1914' (DPhil. thesis, University of Sussex, 1974); Eley, 'Reshaping the Right: Radical Nationalism and the German Navy League, 1898–1908', *The Historical Journal* 21 (1978), 327–54.

4 See, for example, Charles Tilly, *Big Structures, Large Processes, Huge Comparisons* (New York, 1984); Richard E. Lee (ed.), *The Longue Durée and World-Systems Analysis* (Albany, NY, 2012).

5 David Blackbourn and Geoff Eley, *Mythen deutscher Geschichtsschreibung. Die gescheiterte bürgerliche Revolution von 1848* (Frankfurt, 1980); Blackbourn and Eley, *The Peculiarities of German History: Bourgeois Society and Politics in Nineteenth-Century Germany* (Oxford, 1984).

6 Geoff Eley, 'Holocaust History', *London Review of Books* (3 March 1983), 6–9.

7 Gerald Bloom, 'Science and Technology for Health: Towards Universal Access in a Changing World', 2009: http://opendocs.ids.ac.uk/opendocs/handle/123456789/2282; Adrian Ely and Martin Bell, 'The Original "Sussex Manifesto": Its Past and Future Relevance', 2009: http://opendocs.ids.ac.uk/opendocs/handle/123456789/2283; Melissa Leach, 'Sustainability, Development, Social Justice: Towards a New Politics of Innovation', in Leach, *Technologies and Innovations for Development* (Springer, 2012), 19–29; Esha Shah, 'Manifesting Utopia: History and Philosophy of UN Debates on Science and Technology for Sustainable Development': 2009: http://mobile.opendocs.ids.ac.uk/opendocs/handle/123456789/2451.

8 William Robbins, 'William Appleman Williams: "Doing History Is Best of All. No Regrets"', in Lloyd Gardner (ed.), *Redefining the Past: Essays in Diplomatic History in Honor of William Appleman Williams* (Corvallis, OR, 1986), 4–5; Michael D. Bess, 'E. P. Thompson: The Historian as Activist', *The American Historical Review* 98 (1993), 18–38.

9 E. J. Hobsbawm, 'The Social Function of the Past: Some Questions', *Past & Present* 55 (May 1972), 3–17; Hobsbawm, 'Mass-Producing Traditions: Europe, 1870-1914', in E. J. Hobsbawm and T. O. Ranger (eds.), *The Invention of Tradition* (Cambridge, 1983), 263–307.

10 Paul Goodman, 'The Devolution of Democracy', *Dissent* 9 (1962), 10, quoted in Kevin Mattson, *Intellectuals in Action: The Origins of the New Left and Radical Liberalism, 1945–1970* (University Park, PA, 2002), 124.

11 Eley, *A Crooked Line*, 129–30.

12 Lori Thurgood, Mary J. Golladay, and Susan T. Hill, 'US Doctorates in the 20th Century: Special Report' (National Science Foundation, June 2006), 7: www.nsf.gov/statistics/nsf06319/pdf/nsf06319.pdf.

13 Frederick Jackson Turner, *The Character and Influence of the Indian Trade in Wisconsin: A Study of the Trading Post as an Institution* (Baltimore, 1891); W. E. B. Du Bois, 'Suppression of the African Slave Trade in the United States' (PhD dissertation, Harvard University, 1895); Du Bois, *The Suppression of the African Slave-Trade to the United States of America, 1638–1870* (New York, 1896).

14 Benjamin Schmidt, 'What Years Do Historians Write About?', *Sapping Attention* (9 May 2013): http://sappingattention.blogspot.com/2013/05/what-years-do-historians-write-about.html. Our thanks to Ben Schmidt for sharing an updated version of his findings with us and for allowing us to use his visualisation of trends in doctoral theses.

15 Gareth Stedman Jones, *Outcast London: A Study in the Relationship between Classes in Victorian Society* (Oxford, 1971); Stedman Jones, *Languages of Class: Studies in English Working Class History, 1832–1982* (Cambridge, 1983); David R. Roediger, *Wages of Whiteness: Race and the Making of the American Working Class* (London, 1991).

16 Arlette Farge, *Le Goût de l'archive* (Paris, 1989).

17 For example, R. B. Rose, 'The Priestley Riots of 1791', *Past & Present* 18 (1960), 68–88; John Bohstedt, *Riots and Community Politics in England and Wales, 1790–1810* (Cambridge, MA, 1983); Colin Haydon, *Anti-Catholicism in Eighteenth-Century England, c. 1714–80* (Manchester, 1993); Ian Haywood and John Seed (eds.), *The Gordon Riots: Politics, Culture and Insurrection in Late Eighteenth-Century Britain* (Cambridge, 2012).

18 Ilza Veith, *Hysteria: The History of a Disease* (Chicago, 1965); Robert Darnton, *Mesmerism and the End of the Enlightenment in France* (Cambridge, MA, 1968); William J. McGrath, *Freud's Discovery of Psychoanalysis: The Politics of Hysteria* (Ithaca, 1986); Ian Hacking, *Mad Travelers: Reflections on the Reality of Transient Mental Illnesses* (Charlottesville, VA, 1998); Rachel Maines, *The Technology of Orgasm: 'Hysteria', the Vibrator, and Women's Sexual Satisfaction* (Baltimore, 1998); Georges Didi-Huberman, *Invention of Hysteria: Charcot and the Photographic Iconography of the Salpêtrière* (trans.) Alisa Hartz (Cambridge, MA, 2003); David Trotter, 'The Invention of Agoraphobia', *Victorian Literature and Culture* 32 (2004), 463–74; Mark S. Micale, *Hysterical Men: The Hidden History of Male Nervous Illness* (Cambridge, MA, 2008).

19 Eley, *A Crooked Line*, 184, 129.

20 Natalie Zemon Davis, *Society and Culture in Early Modern France: Eight Essays* (Stanford, 1975); Robert Darnton, *The Great Cat Massacre and Other Episodes in French Cultural History* (New York, 1984).

21 Edoardo Grendi, 'Micro-analisi e storia sociale', *Quaderni storici* 35 (1977), 512. See, more generally, Jacques Revel (ed.), *Jeux d'échelles. La micro-analyse à l'expérience* (Paris, 1996); Paola Lanaro (ed.), *Microstoria. A venticinque anni de l'eredità immateriale* (Milan, 2011); Francesca Trivellato, 'Is There a Future for Italian Micro-History in the Age of Global History?', *California Italian Studies* 2 (2011): www.escholarship. org/uc/item/0z94n9hq.

22 Carlo Ginzburg, *Storia notturna. Una decifrazione del sabba* (Turin, 1989).

23 Giovanni Levi, 'On Micro-history', in Peter Burke (ed.), *New Perspectives on Historical Writing* (Cambridge, 1991), 94.

24 Mark Salber Phillips, *On Historical Distance* (New Haven, 2013), 205–6.

25 Richard Rorty (ed.), *The Linguistic Turn: Recent Essays in Philosophical Method* (Chicago, 1967); Gabrielle M. Spiegel (ed.), *Practicing History: New Directions in Historical Writing after the Linguistic Turn* (London, 2005); Judith Surkis, 'When Was the Linguistic Turn? A Genealogy', *American Historical Review* 117 (2012), 700–22.

26 Victoria E. Bonnell and Lynn Hunt (eds.), *Beyond the Cultural Turn: New Directions in the Study of Society and Culture* (Berkeley, 1999); James W. Cook, Lawrence B. Glickman, and Michael O'Malley (eds.), *The Cultural Turn in US History: Past, Present, and Future* (Chicago, 2005).

27 Antoinette Burton (ed.), *After the Imperial Turn: Thinking With and Through the Nation* (Durham, NC, 2003); Ulf Hedetoft, *The Global Turn: National Encounters with the World* (Aalborg, 2003); Winfried Fluck, Donald E. Pease, and John Carlos Rowe (eds.), *Re-Framing the Transnational Turn in American Studies* (Hanover, NH, 2011); Durba Ghosh, 'Another Set of Imperial Turns?', *American Historical Review* 117 (2012), 772–93.

28 Jo Guldi, 'What is the Spatial Turn?' (2011): http://spatial.scholarslab. org/spatial-turn/; David Armitage, 'The International Turn in Intellectual History', in Armitage, *Foundations of Modern International Thought* (Cambridge, 2013), 17–32; also in Darrin M. McMahon and Samuel Moyn (eds.), *Rethinking Modern European Intellectual History* (New York, 2014), 232–52.

29 Judith Surkis, Gary Wilder, James W. Cook, Durba Ghosh, Julia Adeney Thomas, and Nathan Perl-Rosenthal, '*AHR* Forum: Historiographic "Turns" in Critical Perspective', *American Historical Review* 117 (2013), 698–813.

30 Emile Perreau-Saussine, 'Quentin Skinner in Context', *Review of Politics* 69 (2007), 110.

31 Quentin Skinner, 'Introduction: The Return of Grand Theory', in Skinner (ed.), *The Return of Grand Theory in the Human Sciences* (Cambridge, 1985), 12.

32 Quentin Skinner, 'The Vocabulary of Renaissance Republicanism: A Cultural *longue-durée*?', in Alison Brown (ed.), *Language and Images of Renaissance Italy* (Oxford, 1995), 87–110, pointed towards Skinner,

Reason and Rhetoric in the Philosophy of Hobbes (Cambridge, 1996); Skinner, *Liberty Before Liberalism* (Cambridge, 1998); Skinner and Martin van Gelderen (eds.), *Republicanism: A Shared European Heritage*, 2 vols. (Cambridge, 2002); Skinner, 'A Genealogy of the Modern State', *Proceedings of the British* Academy 162 (2009), 325–70; and Skinner and van Gelderen (eds.), *Freedom and the Construction of Europe*, 2 vols. (Cambridge, 2013). Compare Darrin M. McMahon, 'The Return of the History of Ideas?', in McMahon and Moyn (eds.), *Rethinking Modern European Intellectual History*, 13–31; Armitage, 'What's the Big Idea?'.

33 David Knowles, *The Historian and Character* (Cambridge, 1955).

34 John Emerich Edward Dalberg Acton, *Lectures on Modern History* (London, 1906), 14.

35 Elie Halévy, *Histoire du peuple anglais au XIXᵉ siècle*, 1: *L'Angleterre en 1815* (Paris, 1913); Robert Graves, *The Long Week-End: A Social History of Great Britain, 1918–1939* (London, 1940).

36 Kingsley Amis, *Lucky Jim* (1953) (New York, 2012), 9; David Cannadine, 'British History: Past, Present – and Future?', *Past and Present* 116 (1987), 177.

37 E. P. Thompson, *The Making of the English Working Class* (London, 1963); Eugene D. Genovese, *Roll, Jordan, Roll: The World the Slaves Made* (New York, 1974).

38 Joan Wallach Scott, *The Glassworkers of Carmaux: French Craftsmen and Political Action in a Nineteenth-Century City* (Cambridge, MA, 1974); William Sewell, Jr, *Work and Revolution in France: The Language of Labor from the Old Regime to 1848* (Cambridge, 1980).

39 Michel Foucault, *Discipline and Punish: The Birth of the Prison* (trans.) Alan Sheridan (New York, 1979); Jürgen Habermas, *The Structural Transformation of the Public Sphere: An Inquiry into a Category of Bourgeois Society* (trans.) Thomas Burger with the assistance of Frederick Lawrence (Cambridge, MA, 1989).

40 Thomas Laqueur, *Making Sex: Body and Gender from the Greeks to Freud* (Cambridge, MA, 1990); Theodore M. Porter, *Trust in Numbers: The Pursuit of Objectivity in Science and Public Life* (Princeton, NJ, 1995); Miles Ogborn, *Spaces of Modernity: London's Geographies, 1680–1780* (London, 1998); Vanessa R. Schwartz, *Spectacular Realities: Early Mass Culture in Fin-de-Siècle Paris* (Berkeley, 1998).

41 Florence N. McCoy, *Researching and Writing in History: A Practical Handbook for Students* (Berkeley, 1974), 3–6.

42 Paul Bew, *Land and the National Question in Ireland, 1858–82* (Atlantic Highlands, NJ, 1979); L. M. Cullen, 'Review', *The Agricultural History Review* 28 (1980), 140.

43 Rodney Barker, *Political Ideas in Modern Britain: In and After the Twentieth Century* (London, 1978); Leon D. Epstein, 'Review', *Albion: A Quarterly Journal Concerned with British Studies* 11 (1979), 189–90.

44 Arthur Schlesinger, Sr, *The Rise of the City, 1878–98* (New York, 1933); Donald Fleming *et al.*, 'Arthur Meier Schlesinger: February 27, 1888–October 30, 1965', *The Journal of Negro History* 5 (1967), 147.

45 Daniel T. Rodgers, *Age of Fracture* (Cambridge, MA, 2011), 255.

46 Bernard Bailyn, 'The Challenge of Modern Historiography', *American Historical Review* 87 (1982), 2, 4, 7–8.

47 R. R. Palmer, 'A Century of French History in America', *French Historical Studies* 14 (1985), 173–4; David Armitage, 'Foreword', in Palmer, *The Age of the Democratic Revolution: A Political History of Europe and America, 1760–1800*, new edn (Princeton, NJ, 2014), xv–xxii.

48 Cannadine, 'British History: Past, Present – And Future?', 176, 177.

49 Peter Novick, *That Noble Dream: The 'Objectivity Question' and the American Historical Profession* (Cambridge, 1988), 577–92; Jean-François Lyotard, *La Condition postmoderne. Rapport sur le savoir* (Paris, 1979), 7.

50 Jean Heffer, 'Is the *Longue Durée* Un-American?', *Review* 24 (2001), 137.

51 William A. Green, 'Periodization in European and World History', *Journal of World History* 3 (1992), 13.

52 Rebecca Amato and Jeffrey T. Manuel, 'Using Radical Public History Tours to Reframe Urban Crime', *Radical History Review*, 113 (2012), 212–24; Jo Guldi, 'Landscape and Place', in Simon Gunn and Lucy Faire (eds.), *Research Methods for History* (Edinburgh, 2012), 66–80.

53 Jared Diamond, *Collapse: How Societies Choose to Fail or Succeed* (London, 2005); A. J. P. Taylor, *The Origins of the Second World War* (London, 1961), 102.

54 Jason Long, 'Rural–Urban Migration and Socio-economic Mobility in Victorian Britain', *The Journal of Economic History* 65 (2005), 1–35; Long, 'The Surprising Social Mobility of Victorian Britain', *European Review of Economic History* 17 (2013), 1–23; Joel Mokyr, 'Entrepreneurship and the Industrial Revolution in Britain', in David S. Landes, Joel Mokyr, and William J. Baumol, eds., *The Invention of Enterprise: Entrepreneurship from Ancient Mesopotamia to Modern Times* (Princeton, NJ, 2012), 183–210; Andrew Godley and Mark Casson, 'History of Entrepreneurship: Britain, 1900–2000', in Landes, Mokyr, and Baumol, eds., *The Invention of Enterprise*, 243–72.

55 Patrick Joyce, *Work, Society, and Politics: The Culture of the Factory in Later Victorian England* (Brighton, 1980); Gareth Stedman Jones, *Languages of Class: Studies in English Working Class History, 1832–1982* (Cambridge, 1983); Joyce, *Visions of the People: Industrial England and the Question of Class, 1848–1914* (Cambridge, 1991); James Vernon, *Politics and the People: A Study in English Political Culture, c. 1815–1867* (New York, 1993); James Epstein, *Radical Expression: Political Language, Ritual, and Symbol in England, 1790–1850* (New York, 1994); Epstein, *In Practice: Studies in the Language and Culture of Popular Politics in Modern Britain* (Stanford, 2003).

56 David R. Green, 'Pauper Protests: Power and Resistance in Early Nineteenth-Century London Workhouses', *Social History* 31 (2006), 137–59; Green, *Pauper Capital London and the Poor Law, 1790–1870* (Farnham, 2010); David Englander, *Poverty and Poor Law Reform in Nineteenth-Century Britain, 1834–1914: From Chadwick to Booth* (London, 2013).

57 Philip T. Hoffman *et al.*, 'Real Inequality in Europe Since 1500', *The Journal of Economic History* 62 (2002), 322–55.

58 Gareth Stedman Jones, *Outcast London: A Study in the Relationship Between Classes in Victorian Society* (Oxford, 1971).

59 Johnson and Nicholas, 'Male and Female Living Standards in England and Wales, 1812–1867', 470–81; Robert J. Barro, 'Democracy and Growth', *Journal of Economic Growth* 1 (1996), 1–27; Jakob B. Madsen, James B. Ang, and Rajabrata Banerjee, 'Four Centuries of British Economic Growth: The Roles of Technology and Population', *Journal of Economic Growth* 15 (2010), 263–90; Morgan Kelly and Cormac Ó Gráda, 'Numerare Est Errare: Agricultural Output and Food Supply in England Before and During the Industrial Revolution', *The Journal of Economic History* 73 (2013), 1132–63.

60 R. M Hartwell, 'The Rising Standard of Living in England, 1800–1850', *The Economic History Review* 13 (1961), 397–416.

61 Sara Horrell, David Meredith, and Deborah Oxley, 'Measuring Misery: Body Mass, Ageing and Gender Inequality in Victorian London', *Explorations in Economic History* 46 (2009), 93–119; Sébastien Rioux, 'Capitalism and the Production of Uneven Bodies: Women, Motherhood and Food Distribution in Britain *c.* 1850–1914', *Transactions of the Institute of British Geographers*, (2014): doi:10.1111/tran.12063.

62 Sara Horrell, 'The Wonderful Usefulness of History', *The Economic Journal* 113 (2003), F180–F186.

63 Karl Gunnar Persson, 'The Malthus Delusion', *European Review of Economic History* 12 (2008), 165–73.

CHAPTER 3 THE LONG AND THE SHORT: CLIMATE CHANGE,
GOVERNANCE, AND INEQUALITY SINCE THE 1970S

1 Garrett Hardin, 'The Tragedy of the Commons', *Science* 162 (1968), 1243–8; David Feeny *et al.*, 'The Tragedy of the Commons: Twenty-Two Years Later', *Human Ecology* 18 (1990), 1–19; Hardin, 'Extensions of "The Tragedy of the Commons"', *Science* 280 (1998), 682–3.

2 Harrison Brown, *The Challenge of Man's Future* (New York, 1954); Georg Borgstrom, *The Hungry Planet* (New York, 1965); Paul Ehrlich, *The Population Bomb* (New York, 1968); Matthew Connelly, *Fatal*

Misconception: The Struggle to Control World Population (Cambridge, MA, 2008); Alison Bashford, *Global Population: History, Geopolitics, and Life of Earth* (New York, 2014).

3 Janine Delaunay (ed.), *Halte à la Croissance? Enquête sur le Club de Rome* (Paris, 1972); Donella H. Meadows, Dennis L. Meadows, Jorgen Randers, and William W. Behrens, III, *The Limits to Growth* (New York, 1972); Fernando Elichigority, *Planet Management: Limits to Growth, Computer Simulation, and the Emergence of Global Spaces* (Evanston, 1999); Clément Levallois, 'Can De-Growth Be Considered a Policy Option? A Historical Note on Nicholas Georgescu-Roegen and the Club of Rome', *Ecological Economics* 69 (2010), 2272; Josh Eastin, Reiner Grundmann, and Aseem Prakash, 'The Two Limits Debates: "Limits to Growth" and Climate Change', *Futures* 43 (2011), 16–26.

4 Hal Lindsay, *The Late Great Planet Earth* (Grand Rapids, MI, 1970); Daniel Wojcik, 'Embracing Doomsday: Faith, Fatalism, and Apocalyptic Beliefs in the Nuclear Age', *Western Folklore* 55 (1996), 305; Karl Butzer and George Endfield, 'Critical Perspectives on Historical Collapse', *Proceedings of the National Academy of Science* 109 (2012), 3628–31.

5 Martin Rees, *Our Final Century?: Will the Human Race Survive the Twenty-first Century?* (London, 2003), published in the United States as Rees, *Our Final Hour: A Scientist's Warning: How Terror, Error, and Environmental Disaster Threaten Humankind's Future in This Century – On Earth and Beyond* (New York, 2003); Jared Diamond, *Collapse: How Societies Choose to Fail or Succeed* (London, 2005); Vaclav Smil, *Global Catastrophes and Trends: The Next 50 Years* (Cambridge, MA, 2008); James Lovelock, *The Vanishing Face of Gaia: A Final Warning* (New York, 2009); Ian Sample, 'World Faces "Perfect Storm" of Problems by 2030, Chief Scientist to Warn', *Guardian* (18 March 2009): hwww.guardian.co.uk/science/2009/mar/18/perfect-storm-john-beddington-energy-food-climate; David R. Montgomery, *Dirt: The Erosion of Civilizations* (Berkeley, 2012).

6 Clark A. Miller, 'Climate Science and the Making of a Global Political Order', in Sheila Jasanoff (ed.), *States of Knowledge: The Co-Production of Science and Social Order* (London, 2004), 46–66; Naomi Oreskes, 'The Scientific Consensus on Climate Change', *Science* 306 (2004), 1686; Mike Hulme, 'Reducing the Future to Climate: A Story of Climate Determinism and Reductionism', *Osiris* 26 (2011), 245–66; R. Agnihotri and K. Dutta, 'Anthropogenic Climate Change: Observed Facts, Projected Vulnerabilities and Knowledge Gaps', in R. Sinha and R. Ravindra (eds.), *Earth System Processes and Disaster Management* (Berlin, 2013), 123–37.

7 Hulme, in particular, has accused the climate science community of 'climate reductionism' in its accounts of historical agency: Richard Peet,

'The Social Origins of Environmental Determinism', *Annals of the Association of American Geographers* 75 (1985), 309–33; David N. Livingstone, 'Race, Space and Moral Climatology: Notes toward a Genealogy', *Journal of Historical Geography* 28 (2002), 159–80; Christopher D. Merrett, 'Debating Destiny: Nihilism or Hope in Guns, Germs, and Steel?', *Antipode* 35 (2003), 801–6; Andrew Sluyter, 'Neo-Environmental Determinism, Intellectual Damage Control, and Nature/Society Science', *Antipode* 35 (2003), 813–17; Christina R. Foust and William O'Shannon Murphy, 'Revealing and Reframing Apocalyptic Tragedy in Global Warming Discourse', *Environmental Communication* 32 (2009), 151–67; Hulme, 'Reducing the Future to Climate', 246.

8 Nicholas Stern *et al.*, *The Economics of Climate Change: The Stern Review* (Cambridge, 2007); William D. Nordhaus, 'A Review of the "Stern Review on the Economics of Climate Change"', *Journal of Economic Literature* 45 (2007), 686; 'No Need to Panic About Global Warming', *Wall Street Journal*, 27 January 2012, sec. Opinion: http://online.wsj.com/news/articles/SB10001424052970204301404577171531838421366?mg=reno64-wsj&url=http%3A%2F%2Fonline.wsj.com%2Farticle%2FSB10001424052970204301404577171531838421366.html.

9 Gene M. Grossman and Alan B. Krueger, *Economic Growth and the Environment*, National Bureau of Economic Research, Working Paper 4634 (1994): http://www.nber.org/papers/w4634; Nemat Shafik, 'Economic Development and Environmental Quality: An Econometric Analysis', *Oxford Economic Papers* 46 (1994), 757–73; Bjørn Lomborg, *The Skeptical Environmentalist: Measuring the Real State of the World* (Cambridge, 2001). Grossman and Krueger's long-term world-view that "societies have shown remarkable ingenuity in harnessing new technologies" (ibid., p. 1) is grounded in the optimistic history of industrialisation characteristic of David Landes and Joel Mokyr.

10 See, for example, Richard E. Neustadt and Ernest R. May, *Thinking in Time: The Uses of History for Decision-Makers* (New York, 1986); C. A. Bayly, Vijayendra Rao, Simon Szreter, and Michael Woolcock (eds.), *History, Historians and Development Policy: A Necessary Dialogue* (Manchester, 2011).

11 Paul J. Crutzen, 'Geology of Mankind', *Nature*, 415 (2002), 23; Will Steffen, Paul J. Crutzen, and John R. McNeill, 'The Anthropocene: Are Humans Now Overwhelming the Great Forces of Nature?', *AMBIO: A Journal of the Human Environment* 36 (2007), 614–21; Steffen, J. Grinevald, Paul J. Crutzen, and John R. McNeill, 'The Anthropocene: Conceptual and Historical Perspectives', *Philosophical Transactions of the Royal Society A: Mathematical, Physical and Engineering Sciences* 369 (2011), 842–67.

12 Libby Robin, 'Histories for Changing Times: Entering the Anthropocene?', *Australian Historical Studies* 44 (2013), 330.

13 Erle C. Ellis and N. Ramankutty, 'Putting People in the Map: Anthropogenic Biomes of the World', *Frontiers in Ecology and the Environment* 6 (2008), 439–47; Jed O. Kaplan, Kristen M. Krumhardt, Erle C. Ellis, William F. Ruddiman, Carsten Lemmen, and Kees Klein Goldewijk, 'Holocene Carbon Emissions as a Result of Anthropogenic Land Cover Change', *The Holocene* 21 (2011), 775–91. See also *Integrated History and Future of People on Earth* (IHOPE), a project of climate scientists joined by humanists to integrate the story of long time-scales climate change: ihope.org.

14 Frank Biermann, '"Earth System Governance" as a Crosscutting Theme of Global Change Research', *Global Environmental Change* 17 (2007), 326–37; Frank Biermann and Ingrid Boas, 'Preparing for a Warmer World: Towards a Global Governance System to Protect Climate Refugees', *Global Environmental Politics* 10 (2010), 60–88; Biermann *et al.*, 'Navigating the Anthropocene: Improving Earth System Governance', *Science* 335 (2012), 1306–7: http://ie.environment.arizona.edu/files/env/Biermann%20et%20al_2012_Science_Anthropocene.pdf.

15 Chi-Jen Yang and Michael Oppenheimer, 'A "Manhattan Project" for Climate Change?', *Climatic Change* 80 (2007), 199–204; Larry Lohmann, 'Carbon Trading, Climate Justice and the Production of Ignorance: Ten Examples', *Development* 51 (2008), 359–65; Jaap C. J. Kwadijk *et al.*, 'Using Adaptation Tipping Points to Prepare for Climate Change and Sea Level Rise: A Case Study in the Netherlands', *Wiley Interdisciplinary Reviews: Climate Change* 1 (2010), 729–40.

16 Kees Klein Goldewijk, 'Estimating Global Land Use Change over the Past 300 Years: The HYDE Database', *Global Biogeochemical Cycles* 15 (2001), 417–33; Goldewijk, 'Three Centuries of Global Population Growth: A Spatial Referenced Population (Density) Database for 1700–2000', *Population and Environment* 26 (2005), 343–67; Erle C. Ellis *et al.*, 'Anthropogenic Transformation of the Biomes, 1700 to 2000', *Global Ecology and Biogeography* 19 (2010), 589–606; Goldewijk *et al.*, 'The HYDE 3.1 Spatially Explicit Database of Human-Induced Global Land-Use Change over the Past 12,000 Years', *Global Ecology and Biogeography* 20 (2011), 73–86; Erle C. Ellis *et al.*, 'Used Planet: A Global History', *Proceedings of the National Academy of Sciences* 110 (2013), 7978–85.

17 Anil Markandya, 'Can Climate Change Be Reversed under Capitalism?', *Development and Change* 40 (2009), 1141.

18 David I. Stern and Michael S. Common, 'Is There an Environmental Kuznets Curve for Sulfur?', *Journal of Environmental Economics and Management* 41 (2001), 162–78; Stern 'The Rise and Fall of the Environmental Kuznets Curve', *World Development* 32 (2004), 1419–39.

19 Historians of Germany have documented a crisis in wood that spread through early-modern Europe and propelled the search for new colonies with unfelled timber to exploit, and later coal and oil to burn. Their work has involved examining the court records of dozens of local vicinities across Germany, documenting when and under what conditions peasants received the maximum punishment possible for chopping down trees that were not their own. Paul Warde, 'Fear of Wood Shortage and the Reality of the Woodland in Europe, *c.* 1450–1850', *History Workshop Journal* 62 (2006), 28–57; Warde, *Ecology, Economy and State Formation in Early Modern Germany* (Cambridge, 2006). More generally, see Astrid Kander, Paolo Manamina, and Paul Warde, *Power to the People: Energy in Europe over the Last Five Centuries* (Princeton, NJ, 2014).

20 Terje Tvedt, *The River Nile in the Age of the British: Political Ecology and the Quest for Economic Power* (London, 2004); Terje Tvedt *et al.*, *A History of Water*, 3 vols. (London, 2006); Tvedt, Terje Oestigaard, and Richard Coopey, *A History of Water, Series ii*, 3 vols. (London, 2010).

21 Terje Tvedt, *A Journey in the Future of Water* (London, 2014).

22 Sabine Barles, 'Feeding the City: Food Consumption and Flow of Nitrogen, Paris, 1801–1914', *Science of the Total Environment* 375 (2007), 48–58; Barles and Laurence Lestel, 'The Nitrogen Question: Urbanization, Industrialization, and River Quality in Paris, 1830–1939', *Journal of Urban History* 33 (2007), 794–812; Barles, 'Urban Metabolism of Paris and Its Region', *Journal of Industrial Ecology* 13 (2009), 898–913; Gilles Billen *et al.*, 'The Food-Print of Paris: Long-Term Reconstruction of the Nitrogen Flows Imported into the City from Its Rural Hinterland', *Regional Environmental Change* 9 (2009), 13–24; Billen *et al.*, 'Grain, Meat and Vegetables to Feed Paris: Where Did and Do They Come from? Localising Paris Food Supply Areas from the Eighteenth to the Twenty-First Century', *Regional Environmental Change* 12 (2012), 325–35.

23 Christopher Hamlin, 'Sewage: Waste or Resource?', *Environment: Science and Policy for Sustainable Development* 22 (1980), 16–42; E. Marald, 'Everything Circulates: Agricultural Chemistry and Recycling Theories in the Second Half of the Nineteenth Century', *Environment and History* 8 (2002), 65–84; Timothy Cooper, 'Peter Lund Simmonds and the Political Ecology of Waste Utilization in Victorian Britain', *Technology and Culture* 52 (2011), 21–44; Peter Thorsheim, 'The Corpse in the Garden: Burial, Health, and the Environment in Nineteenth-Century London', *Environmental History* 16 (2011), 38–68.

24 Joan Thirsk, *Alternative Agriculture: A History from the Black Death to the Present Day* (Oxford, 1997); Martin Mulligan and Stuart Hill,

Ecological Pioneers: A Social History of Australian Ecological Thought and Action (Cambridge, 2001); Paul B. Thompson, *The Agrarian Vision: Sustainability and Environmental Ethics* (Lexington, KY, 2010).

25 Robin, 'Histories for Changing Times', 339–40.

26 Joshua J. Yates, 'Abundance on Trial: The Cultural Significance of "Sustainability"', *The Hedgehog Review* 14 (2012), 22.

27 Yates, 'Abundance on Trial', 12.

28 Mulligan and Hill, *Ecological Pioneers*.

29 Anil Agarwal and Sunita Narain, *Global Warming in an Unequal World: A Case of Environmental Colonialism* (New Delhi, 1991); Andreas Malm and Alf Hornborg, 'The Geology of Mankind? A Critique of the Anthropocene Narrative', *The Anthropocene Review* (2014): doi: 10.1177/2053019613516291. For a contrary view on the importance of blame to environmental history, see Paul S. Sutter, 'The World with Us: The State of American Environmental History', *Journal of American History* 100 (2013), 98.

30 James C. Scott, *Seeing Like a State: How Certain Schemes to Improve the Human Condition Have Failed* (New Haven, 1998); Fredrik Albritton Jonsson, *Enlightenment's Frontier: The Scottish Highlands and the Origins of Environmentalism* (New Haven, 2013).

31 Malm and Hornborg, 'The Geology of Mankind?', 3. The quotation included is from John Lewis Gaddis, *The Landscape of History* (Oxford, 2002), 96.

32 Peter Linebaugh, 'Enclosures from the Bottom Up', *Radical History Review* 108 (2010), 11–27; Anant Maringanti *et al.*, 'Tragedy of the Commons Revisited (1)', *Economic and Political Weekly* 47 (2012), 10–13; Michael Heller, 'The Tragedy of the Anticommons: A Concise Introduction and Lexicon', *The Modern Law Review* 76 (2013), 6–25; Kenneth R. Olwig, 'Globalism and the Enclosure of the Landscape Commons', in Ian D. Rotherham (ed.), *Cultural Severance and the Environment: The Ending of Traditional and Customary Practice on Commons and Landscapes Managed in Common* (Dordrecht, 2013), 31–46. See also the abundant scholarship on the history of the commons in Elinor Ostrom *et al.*, *Digital Library of the Commons*: http://dlc.dlib. indiana.edu/dlc/. Ostrom's own scholarship on the commons was less about historical duration than the derivation of abstract principles that seemed to characterise the best-lasting of these commons. The literature on the enclosure of the European commons is useful to think about here: Leigh Shaw-Taylor, 'Parliamentary Enclosure and the Emergence of an English Agricultural Proletariat', *Journal of Economic History* 61 (2001), 640–62.

33 Marsha L. Weisiger, *Dreaming of Sheep in Navajo Country* (Seattle, 2009).

34 Nathan F. Sayre, 'The Genesis, History, and Limits of Carrying Capacity', *Annals of the Association of American Geographers* 98 (2008), 120–34.

35 Connelly, *Fatal Misconception*; Bashford, *Global Population*.

36 Michael Redclift, 'Sustainable Development (1987–2005): An Oxymoron Comes of Age', *Sustainable Development* 13 (2005), 212–27; Chris Sneddon, Richard B. Howarth, and Richard B. Norgaard, 'Sustainable Development in a Post-Brundtland World', *Ecological Economics* 57 (2006), 253–68; Paul B. Thompson, *The Agrarian Vision: Sustainability and Environmental Ethics* (Lexington, KY, 2010), 197–200.

37 Angus Burgin, *The Great Persuasion: Reinventing Free Markets Since the Depression* (Cambridge, MA, 2012).

38 David Harvey, *A Brief History of Neoliberalism* (Oxford, 2005); Wolfgang Streeck, *Buying Time: The Delayed Crisis of Democratic Capitalism* (London, 2014).

39 Eric Schmidt and Jared Cohen, *The New Digital Age: Transforming Nations, Businesses, and Our Lives* (New York, 2014).

40 Francis Fukuyama, *The End of History and the Last Man* (New York, 1992); Samuel P. Huntington, *The Clash of Civilizations and the Remaking of World Order* (New York, 1996).

41 Errol Henderson, 'Culture or Contiguity? Ethnic Conflict, the Similarity of States, and the Onset of Interstate War, 1820–1989', *Journal of Conflict Resolution* 41 (1997), 649–68; Henderson, 'The Democratic Peace through the Lens of Culture, 1820–1989', *International Studies Quarterly* 42 (1998), 461–84; Manus I. Midlarsky, 'Democracy and Islam: Implications for Civilizational Conflict and the Democratic Peace', *International Studies Quarterly* 42 (1998), 485–511; Eric Weede, 'Islam and the West: How Likely Is a Clash of These Civilizations?', *International Review of Sociology* 8 (1998), 183–95; Bruce M. Russett, John R. Oneal, and Michaelene Cox, 'Clash of Civilizations, or Realism and Liberalism Déjà Vu? Some Evidence', *Journal of Peace Research* 37 (2000), 583–608; Giacomo Chiozza, 'Is There a Clash of Civilizations? Evidence from Patterns of International Conflict Involvement, 1946–97', *Journal of Peace Research* 39 (2002), 711–34; Tanja Ellingsen, 'Toward a Revival of Religion and Religious Clashes?', *Terrorism and Political Violence* 17 (2005), 305–32; Kunihiko Imai, 'Culture, Civilization, or Economy? Test of the Clash of Civilizations Thesis', *International Journal on World Peace* 23 (2006), 3–26; Mustafa Aydin and Çınar Özen, 'Civilizational Futures: Clashes or Alternative Visions in the Age of Globalization?', *Futures*, Special Issue: Futures for Multiple Civilizations, 42 (2010), 545–52; Alexis Pasichny, 'Two Methods of Analysis for Huntington's "Clash of Civilizations"', *Challenges of Modern Technology* 3 (2012): http://yadda.icm.edu.pl/baztech/element/

bwmetaɪ.element.baztech-ddff88f7-7650-49d5-8164-033422b0deɪe/c/
Pasichny.pdf.

42 Shireen Hunter and Huma Malik, *Modernization, Democracy, and Islam* (Westport, CT, 2005).

43 David Graeber, *Debt: The First 5,000 Years* (Brooklyn, NY, 2010).

44 David Armitage, *The Declaration of Independence: A Global History* (Cambridge, MA, 2007); Andreas Wimmer and Yuval Feinstein, 'The Rise of the Nation-State Across the World, 1816 to 2001', *American Sociological Review* 75 (2010), 764–90.

45 Michael Goldman, *Imperial Nature: The World Bank and Struggles for Social Justice in the Age of Globalization* (New Haven, 2005); Amy L. Sayward, *The Birth of Development: How the World Bank, Food and Agriculture Organization, and World Health Organization Changed the World, 1945–1965* (Kent, OH, 2006); Mark Mazower, *Governing the World: The History of an Idea* (London, 2012); Patricia Clavin, *Securing the World Economy: The Reinvention of the League of Nations, 1920–1946* (Oxford, 2013).

46 Angus Lindsay Wright, *To Inherit the Earth: The Landless Movement and the Struggle for a New Brazil* (Oakland, CA, 2003); Wendy Wolford, *This Land Is Ours Now: Social Mobilization and the Meanings of Land in Brazil* (Durham, NC, 2010).

47 Jo Guldi, *Roads to Power: Britain Invents the Infrastructure State* (Cambridge, MA, 2012).

48 Fred Turner, *From Counterculture to Cyberculture: Stewart Brand, the Whole Earth Network, and the Rise of Digital Utopianism* (Chicago, 2006); Matthew Hilton, 'Politics Is Ordinary: Non-Governmental Organizations and Political Participation in Contemporary Britain', *Twentieth Century British History* 22 (2011), 230–68; Jo Guldi, 'Can Participatory Maps Save the World?' (talk at Brown University, 7 November 2013): https://www.youtube.com/watch?v=tYL4pVUW7 Lg&list=PLTiEffrOcz_7MwEs7L79ocdSIVhuLXM22&index=ɪɪ.

49 Penny Summerfield, 'Mass-Observation: Social Research or Social Movement?', *Journal of Contemporary History* 20 (1985), 439–52; David Matless, 'Regional Surveys and Local Knowledges: The Geographical Imagination in Britain, 1918–39', *Transactions of the Institute of British Geographers*, New Series, 17 (1992), 464–80; Matless, 'The Uses of Cartographic Literacy: Mapping, Survey and Citizenship in Twentieth-Century Britain', in Dennis E. Cosgrove (ed.), *Mappings* (London, 1999), 193–212; James Hinton, *The Mass Observers: A History, 1937–1949* (Oxford, 2013).

50 David Ludden, 'Patronage and Irrigation in Tamil Nadu: A Long-Term View', *Indian Economic & Social History Review* 16 (1979), 347–65; Christopher Hamlin, *Public Health and Social Justice in the Age of Chadwick: Britain, 1800–1854* (Cambridge, 1998); Timothy Mitchell,

Rule of Experts: Egypt, Techno-Politics, Modernity (Berkeley, 2002); Rohan D'Souza, *Drowned and Damned: Colonial Capitalism and Flood Control in Eastern India* (New Delhi, 2006).

51 Terje Tvedt, 'NGOs' Role at "The End of History": Norwegian Policy and the New Paradigm', *Forum for Development Studies* 21 (1994), 139–66; J. Petras, 'Imperialism and NGOs in Latin America', *Monthly Review – New York* 49 (1997), 10–27; Akira Iriye, 'A Century of NGOs', *Diplomatic History* 23 (1999), 421–35; Diana Mitlin, Sam Hickey, and Anthony Bebbington, 'Reclaiming Development? NGOs and the Challenge of Alternatives', *World Development* 35 (2007), 1699–720.

52 John Markoff and Verónica Montecinos, 'The Ubiquitous Rise of Economists', *Journal of Public Policy* 13 (1993), 37–68; Marion Fourcade, 'The Construction of a Global Profession: The Transnationalization of Economics', *American Journal of Sociology*, 112 (2006), 145–94.

53 Richard White, *Railroaded: The Transcontinentals and the Making of Modern America* (New York, 2011).

54 Nick Cullather, '"The Target Is the People": Representations of the Village in Modernization and US National Security Doctrine', *Cultural Politics: An International Journal* 2 (2006), 29–48; Cullather, 'The Foreign Policy of the Calorie', *The American Historical Review* 112 (2007), 337–64; Greg Grandin, *Fordlandia: The Rise and Fall of Henry Ford's Forgotten Jungle City* (New York, 2009); Cullather, *The Hungry World: America's Cold War Battle Against Poverty in Asia* (Cambridge, MA, 2010).

55 Richard R. Nelson and Sydney G. Winter, *An Evolutionary Theory of Economic Change* (Cambridge, MA, 1982); Nelson and Winter, 'Evolutionary Theorizing in Economics', *Journal of Economic Perspectives* 16 (2002), 23–46.

56 Zachary Karabell, *The Leading Indicators: A Short History of the Numbers that Rule Our World* (New York, 2014), 52–72.

57 Thomas Piketty, *Le Capital au XXIe siècle* (Paris, 2013); Piketty, *Capital in the Twenty-First Century* (trans.) Arthur Goldhammer (Cambridge, MA, 2014).

58 Piketty, *Capital in the Twenty-First Century*, 11–17.

59 Simon Kuznets and Elizabeth Jenks, *Shares of Upper Income Groups in Income and Savings* (Cambridge, MA, 1953); Simon Kuznets, 'Economic Growth and Income Inequality', *American Economic Review* 45 (1955), 1–28.

60 Chris Giles, 'Data Problems with Capital in the 21st Century': http://blogs.ft.com/money-supply/2014/05/23/data-problems-with-capital-in-the-21st-century; Thomas Piketty, 'Technical Appendix of the Book, *Capital in the 21st Century*' (21 May 2014): http://piketty.pse.ens.fr/files/capital21c/en/Piketty2014TechnicalAppendixResponsetoFT.pdf.

61 Ian Hacking, *The Emergence of Probability: A Philosophical Study of Early Ideas About Probability, Induction and Statistical Inference* (Cambridge, 1975); Theodore M. Porter, *The Rise of Statistical Thinking, 1820–1900* (Princeton, NJ, 1986); Ian Hacking, *The Taming of Chance* (Cambridge, 1990); Porter, *Trust in Numbers: The Pursuit of Objectivity in Science and Public Life* (Princeton, NJ, 1995); Alain Desrosières, *The Politics of Large Numbers: A History of Statistical Reasoning* (Cambridge, MA, 2002); Michael Ward, *Quantifying the World: UN Ideas and Statistics* (Bloomington, IN, 2004); Karabell, *The Leading Indicators*.

62 Sebastian De Grazia, *Of Time, Work, and Leisure* (New York, 1962); Ivan Illich, *Toward a History of Needs* (New York, 1978).

63 Facundo Alvaredo, Anthony Atkinson, Thomas Piketty, and Emmanuel Saez, 'The World Top Incomes Database': http://topincomes.parisschoolofeconomics.eu/.

64 Piketty, *Capital in the Twenty-First Century*, 33.

65 Tony Judt, 'A Clown in Regal Purple: Social History and the Historians', *History Workshop Journal* 7 (1979), 84–5 (on Scott and Sewell, among others). Judt was, however, critical of the effects of Braudel's *longue durée* on the 'dismantl[ing] of the historical event altogether. One result of this is a glut of articles about minute and marginal matters': *ibid.*, 85.

66 Quoted by Grace V. Leslie, 'Seven Hundred Pages of "Minor Revisions" from the Soviet Union: Caroline Ware, the UNESCO *History of Mankind*, and the Trials of Writing International History in a Bi-Polar World, 1954–66', paper presented at the annual meeting of the American Historical Association, New Orleans, Louisiana, 3 January 2013; on the UNESCO project more generally, see Gilbert Allardyce, 'Toward World History: American Historians and the Coming of the World History Course', *Journal of World History* 1 (1990), 26–40.

67 Frederick Cooper and Randall M. Packard (eds.), *International Development and the Social Sciences: Essays on the History and Politics of Knowledge* (Berkeley, 1997); Gilbert Rist, *The History of Development: From Western Origins to Global Faith* (New York, 2002); Nils Gilman, *Mandarins of the Future: Modernization Theory in Cold War America* (Baltimore, 2007).

68 Jean-Claude Passeron and Jacques Revel, 'Penser par cas. Raissoner à partir de singularités', in Passeron and Revel (eds.), *Penser par cas* (Paris, 2005), 9–44.

69 Markoff and Montecinos, 'The Ubiquitous Rise of Economists'; Gerald D. Suttles and Mark D. Jacobs, *Front Page Economics* (Chicago, 2011).

70 Elegies for this moment include Russell Jacoby, *The Last Intellectuals: American Culture in the Age of Academe* (New York, 1987); Michael Bérubé and Cary Nelson (eds.), *Higher Education under Fire: Politics,*

Economics, and the Crisis of the Humanities (New York, 1995); Richard A. Posner, *Public Intellectuals: A Study of Decline* (Cambridge, MA, 2003); Jo Guldi, 'The Surprising Death of the Public Intellectual: A Manifesto', *Absent* 1 (2008): http://archive.org/details/TheSurprisingDeathOfThe PublicIntellectualAManifestoForRestoration.

71 Daniel Lord Smail, *On Deep History and the Brain* (Berkeley, 2008); Smail, 'Beyond the *Longue Durée*: Human History and Deep Time', *Perspectives on History*, 50 (2012), 59–60.

72 Denis E. Cosgrove, *Apollo's Eye: A Cartographic Genealogy of the Earth in the Western Imagination* (Baltimore, 2001); John R. Gillis, *The Human Shore: Seacoasts in History* (Chicago, 2012).

73 Constantin Fasolt, *The Limits of History* (Chicago, 2004), 19.

74 Jeremy Adelman, 'Latin American *Longues Durées*', *Latin American Research Review* 39 (2004), 224; Thomas W. Laqueur, 'Sexuality and the Transformation of Culture: The *Longue Durée*', *Sexualities* 12 (2009), 418; Susan Gillman, 'Oceans of *Longues Durées*', *PMLA* 127 (2012), 328.

75 Matthew Connelly, 'The Cold War in the *Longue Durée*: Global Migration, Public Health, and Population Control', in Melvyn P. Leffler and Odd Arne Westad (eds.), *The Cambridge History of the Cold War*, 3 vols. (Cambridge, 2009), III 466–88; William M. Johnston, *Visionen der langen Dauer Österreichs* (Vienna, 2009); Suzanne L. Marchand, 'Orientalism and the *Longue Durée*', in Marchand, *German Orientalism in the Age of Empire: Religion, Race, and Scholarship.* (Cambridge, 2009), 1–52; Laurence Lux-Sterritt and Carmen M. Mangion, 'Gender, Catholicism and Women's Spirituality over the *Longue Durée*', in Lux-Sterritt and Mangion (eds.), *Gender, Catholicism and Spirituality: Women and the Roman Catholic Church in Britain and Europe, 1200–1900* (Basingstoke, 2011), 1–18; Alexander A. Bauer and Owen P. Doonan, 'Fluid Histories: Culture, Community, and the *Longue Durée* of the Black Sea World', in Ruxandra Ivan (ed.), *New Regionalism or No Regionalism?: Emerging Regionalism in the Black Sea Area* (Farnham, 2012), 13–30; Dirk Hoerder, 'Migrations and Belongings: A *Longue-Durée* Perspective', in Emily S. Rosenberg (ed.), *A World Connecting, 1870–1945* (Cambridge, MA, 2012), 444–67; Julia Clancy-Smith, 'From Sidi Bou Zid to Sidi Bou Said: A *Longue Durée* Approach to the Tunisian Revolutions', in Mark L. Haas and David W. Lesch (eds.), *The Arab Spring: Change and Resistance in the Middle East* (Boulder, CO, 2013), 13–34; Jörn Leonhard, 'Introduction: The *Longue Durée* of Empire: Comparative Semantics of a Key Concept in Modern European History', *Contributions to the History of Concepts* 8 (2013), 1–25.

76 Ben Kiernan, *Blood and Soil: A World History of Genocide and Extermination from Sparta to Darfur* (New Haven, 2007); Diarmaid MacCulloch, *A History of Christianity: The First Three Thousand Years* (London, 2009);

Ian Morris, *Why the West Rules – For Now: The Patterns of History, and What They Reveal About the Future* (New York, 2010); Max Boot, *Invisible Armies: An Epic History of Guerrilla Warfare from Ancient Times to the Present* (New York, 2012); Joyce E. Chaplin, *Round About the Earth: Circumnavigation from Magellan to Orbit* (New York, 2012); Lawrence Freedman, *Strategy: A History* (Oxford, 2013); Morris, *The Measure of Civilization: How Social Development Decides the Fate of Nations* (Princeton, 2013); David Nirenberg, *Anti-Judaism: The Western Tradition* (New York, 2013); Francisco Bethencourt, *Racisms: From the Crusades to the Twentieth Century* (Princeton, NJ, 2013).

77 Cynthia Stokes Brown, *Big History: From the Big Bang to the Present* (New York, 2007); Fred Spier, *Big History and the Future of Humanity* (Chichester, 2010); David Christian, *Maps of Time: An Introduction to Big History*, new edn (Berkeley, 2011). The questions treated in Harriet Swain (ed.), *Big Questions in History* (London, 2005), are 'big' in the sense of general, not because they necessarily encompass large expanses of time or space.

78 Andrew Shryock and Daniel Lord Smail (eds.), *Deep History: The Architecture of Past and Present* (Berkeley, 2011); Smail and Shryock, 'History and the *Pre*', *American Historical Review* 118 (2013), 709–37.

79 Dipesh Chakrabarty, 'The Climate of History: Four Theses', *Critical Inquiry* 35 (2009), 197–222; Chakrabarty, 'Postcolonial Studies and the Challenge of Climate Change', *New Literary History* 43 (2012), 1–18; Fredrik Albritton Jonsson, 'The Industrial Revolution in the Anthropocene', *The Journal of Modern History* 84 (2012), 679–96; Alison Bashford, 'The Anthropocene is Modern History: Reflections on Climate and Australian Deep Time', *Australian Historical Studies* 44 (2013), 341–9.

80 James Vernon, *Distant Strangers: How Britain Became Modern* (Berkeley, 2014), 132.

CHAPTER 4 BIG QUESTIONS, BIG DATA

1 Ann Blair, 'Reading Strategies for Coping with Information Overload ca. 1550–1700', *Journal of the History of Ideas* 64 (2003), 11–28; Brian W. Ogilvie, 'The Many Books of Nature: Renaissance Naturalists and Information Overload', *Journal of the History of Ideas* 64 (2003), 29–40; Daniel Rosenberg, 'Early Modern Information Overload', *Journal of the History of Ideas* 64 (2003), 1–9; Ann Blair, *Too Much to Know: Managing Scholarly Information Before the Modern Age* (New Haven, 2010).

2 Prabhakar Raghavan, 'It's Time to Scale the Science in the Social Sciences', *Big Data and Society* 1 (2014): doi:10.1177/2053951714532240.

3 See, for example, David Geggus, 'Sex Ratio, Age and Ethnicity in the Atlantic Slave Trade: Data from French Shipping and Plantation Records', *The Journal of African History* 30 (1989), 23–44; Thomas C. Peterson and Russell S. Vose, 'An Overview of the Global Historical Climatology Network Temperature Database', *Bulletin of the American Meteorological Society* 78 (1997), 2837–49; Stephen C. Trombulak and Richard Wolfson, 'Twentieth-Century Climate Change in New England and New York, USA', *Geophysical Research Letters* 31 (2004), 1–4; Indra De Soysa and Eric Neumayer, 'Resource Wealth and the Risk of Civil War Onset: Results from a New Dataset of Natural Resource Rents, 1970–1999', *Conflict Management and Peace Science* 24 (2007), 201–18; David Eltis, 'The US Transatlantic Slave Trade, 1644–1867: An Assessment', *Civil War History* 54 (2008), 347–78; Nathan Nunn, 'The Long-Term Effects of Africa's Slave Trades', *The Quarterly Journal of Economics* 123 (2008), 139–76; Kenneth E. Kunkel *et al.*, 'Trends in Twentieth-Century US Snowfall Using a Quality-Controlled Dataset', *Journal of Atmospheric and Oceanic Technology* 26 (2009), 33–44; Nathan Nunn and Leonard Wantchekon, *The Slave Trade and the Origins of Mistrust in Africa* (National Bureau of Economic Research, 2009): www.nber.org/papers/w14783; David Eltis and David Richardson, 'The Trans-Atlantic Slave Trade Database Voyages: "Introductory Maps"', Map (Emory University: Digital Library Research Initiative, 1 January 2010): https://saylor.longsight.com/handle/1/12201; Lakshmi Iyer, 'Direct versus Indirect Colonial Rule in India: Long-Term Consequences', *The Review of Economics and Statistics* 92 (2010), 693–713; Adrian M. Lister, 'Natural History Collections as Sources of Long-Term Datasets', *Trends in Ecology & Evolution* 26 (2011), 153–4; Enric Tello and Marc Badía-Miró, 'Land-Use Profiles of Agrarian Income and Land Ownership Inequality in the Province of Barcelona in Mid-Nineteenth Century', January 2011: http://repositori.uji.es/xmlui/handle/10234/20513; Patrick Manning, 'Historical Datasets on Africa and the African Atlantic', *Journal of Comparative Economics, Slavery, Colonialism and Institutions Around the World*, 40 (2012), 604–7; Colin F. Wilder, 'Teaching Old Dogs New Tricks: Four Motifs of Legal Change from Early Modern Europe', *History and Theory* 51 (2012), 18–41; G. S. J. Hawkins *et al.*, 'Data Rescue and Re-Use: Recycling Old Information to Address New Policy Concerns', *Marine Policy* 42 (2013), 91–8.
4 Edward Tufte, *The Visual Display of Quantitative Information*, 2nd edn (Cheshire, CT, 2001); Daniel Rosenberg and Anthony Grafton, *Cartographies of Time* (New York, 2010).
5 Tomiko Yamaguchi and Craig K. Harris, 'The Economic Hegemonization of Bt Cotton Discourse in India', *Discourse & Society* 15 (2004),

467–91; Anabela Carvalho and Jacquelin Burgess, 'Cultural Circuits of Climate Change in UK Broadsheet Newspapers, 1985–2003', *Risk Analysis* 25 (2005), 1457–69; Francis L. F. Lee, Chin-Chuan Lee, and Nina Luzhou Li, 'Chinese Peasants in the Process of Economic Reform: An Analysis of *New York Times*'s and *Washington Post*'s Opinion Discourses, 1981–2008', *Communication, Culture & Critique* 4 (2011), 164–83; Alan Partington, 'The Changing Discourses on Antisemitism in the UK Press from 1993 to 2009: A Modern-Diachronic Corpus-Assisted Discourse Study', *Journal of Language and Politics* 11 (2012), 51–76; Bruno Turnheim and Frank W. Geels, 'Regime Destabilisation as the Flipside of Energy Transitions: Lessons from the History of the British Coal Industry (1913–1997)', *Energy Policy*, Special Section: Past and Prospective Energy Transitions – Insights from History, 50 (2012), 35–49.

6 John Cook *et al.*, 'Quantifying the Consensus on Anthropogenic Global Warming in the Scientific Literature', *Environmental Research Letters* 8 (2013): doi:10.1088/1748-9326/8/2/024024.

7 Brad Pasanek and D. Sculley, 'Mining Millions of Metaphors', *Literary and Linguistic Computing* 23 (2008), 345–60; D. Sculley and Bradley M. Pasanek, 'Meaning and Mining: The Impact of Implicit Assumptions in Data Mining for the Humanities', *Literary and Linguistic Computing* 23 (2008), 409–24; Frederick W. Gibbs and Daniel J. Cohen, 'A Conversation with Data: Prospecting Victorian Words and Ideas', *Victorian Studies* 54 (2011), 69–77; Joanna Guldi, 'The History of Walking and the Digital Turn: Stride and Lounge in London, 1808–1851', *The Journal of Modern History* 84 (2012), 116–44; Matthew Lee Jockers, *Macroanalysis: Digital Methods and Literary History* (Urbana, 2013); Ted Underwood, 'We Don't Already Understand the Broad Outlines of Literary History', *The Stone and the Shell* 8 (2013): http://tedunderwood.com/2013/02/08/we-dont-already-know-the-broad-outlines-of-literary-history/.

8 http://papermachines.org/; www.zotero.org/.

9 Jo Guldi, *The Long Land War: A Global History of Land Reform, c. 1860–Present* (forthcoming).

10 Daniel Rosenberg's work on the Google Books corpus suggests that the reasons for turns in Ngrams have a great deal to do with the corpus selected for Google Books. Nonetheless, Ngrams remain useful for doing transcontinental, transtemporal comparisons, comparing the rise of words like 'holocaust' and 'shoah' across English, German, French, Russian, and Hebrew. But in aggregate, supplemented by other kinds of story-telling, the tools of abstraction and synthesis can also offer insight into the basic events and struggles that gave us the modern world. Geoffrey Nunberg, 'Counting on Google Books', *Chronicle of Higher Education* (16 December 2010): http://chronicle.

com/article/Counting-on-Google-Books/125735; Anthony Grafton, 'Loneliness and Freedom', *AHA Perspectives* (March 2011): www.historians.org/Perspectives/issues/2011/1103/1103pre1.cfm; Erez Aiden and Jean-Baptiste Michel, *Uncharted: Big Data as a Lens on Human Culture* (New York, 2013); Daniel Rosenberg, 'Data Before the Fact', in Lisa Gitelman (ed.), *'Raw Data' Is an Oxymoron* (Cambridge, MA, 2013), 15–40.

11 Franco Moretti, *Graphs, Maps, Trees: Abstract Models for a Literary History* (New York, 2007); Ben Schmidt, *Sapping Attention*: http://sappingattention.blogspot.com/.

12 http://books.google.com/ngrams; www.wordle.net/; http://papermachines.org/.

13 On the billion words of post-classical Latin now available for digital analysis, see David Bamman and David Smith, 'Extracting Two Thousand Years of Latin from a Million Book Library', *Journal on Computing and Cultural Heritage* 5 (2012), 1–13.

14 Michael Friendly, 'A.-M. Guerry's "Moral Statistics of France": Challenges for Multivariable Spatial Analysis', *Statistical Science* 22 (2007), 368–99; Friendly, 'A Brief History of Data Visualization', in Chun-houh Chen, Wolfgang Härdle, and Antony Unwin, *Handbook of Data Visualization* (Berlin, 2008), 15–56; Friendly, Matthew Sigal, and Derek Harnanansingh, 'The Milestones Project: A Database for the History of Data Visualization' (2012): http://datavis.ca/papers/MilestonesProject.pdf.

15 Tim Hitchcock and Robert Shoemaker, 'Digitising History from Below: The Old Bailey Proceedings Online, 1674–1834', *History Compass* 4 (2006), 1–10: www.oldbaileyonline.org/; https://sites.google.com/site/colinwilder/.

16 Central Intelligence Agency, *Potential Implications of Trends in World Population, Food Production and Climate*, Report No. OPR-401 (Washington, DC, 1974); Crispin Tickell, *Climate Change and World Affairs* (Cambridge, MA, 1977), 64; Jill Williams (ed.), *Carbon Dioxide, Climate and Society* (Oxford, 1978); Council of Environmental Quality, *Global Energy Futures and the Carbon Dioxide Problem* (Washington, DC, 1981); Sheila Jasanoff, 'Image and Imagination: The Formation of Global Environmental Conscious-ness', in Clark Miller and Paul N. Edwards (eds.), *Changing the Atmosphere* (Cambridge, MA, 2001), 309–37; Paul N. Edwards, *A Vast Machine: Computer Models, Climate Data, and the Politics of Global Warming* (Cambridge, MA, 2010); Mike Hulme, 'Reducing the Future to Climate: A Story of Climate Determinism and Reductionism', *Osiris* 26 (2011), 245–66.

17 G. van der Schrier *et al.*, 'A scPDSI-Based Global Data Set of Dry and Wet Spells for 1901–2009', *Journal of Geophysical Research: Atmospheres* 118 (2013), 4025–48.

18 Benjamin S. Felzer, 'Carbon, Nitrogen, and Water Response to Climate and Land Use Changes in Pennsylvania During the 20th and 21st Centuries', *Ecological Modelling* 240 (2012), 49–63.

19 C. J. Caseldine and C. Turney, 'The Bigger Picture: Towards Integrating Palaeoclimate and Environmental Data with a History of Societal Change', *Journal of Quaternary Science* 25 (2010), 88–93.

20 Joseph A. Tainter, 'Energy, Complexity, and Sustainability: A Historical Perspective', *Environmental Innovation and Societal Transitions* 1 (2011), 89–95; Geoffrey Parker, *Global Crisis: War, Climate Change and Catastrophe in the Seventeenth Century* (New Haven, 2013); Harry Verhoeven, 'Climate Change, Conflict and Development in Sudan: Global Neo-Malthusian Narratives and Local Power Struggles', *Development and Change* 42 (2011), 679–707.

21 www.eia.gov/totalenergy/data/annual/; http://data.un.org/; www.euromonitor.com; www.imf.org/external/pubs/cat/longres.cfm?sk=18674.0.

22 Robert C. Allen *et al.*, 'Preliminary Global Price Comparisons, 1500–1870', paper presented at the *XIII Congress of the International Economic History Association, Buenos Aires (July 22–26)*, 2002: www.iisg.nl/hpw/papers/lindert.pdf; Livio Di Matteo, 'The Effect of Religious Denomination on Wealth: Who Were the Truly Blessed?', *Social Science History* 31 (2007), 299–341; Kunkel *et al.*, 'Trends in Twentieth-Century US Snowfall', 33–44; W. Bradford Wilcox *et al.*, 'No Money, No Honey, No Church: The Deinstitutionalization of Religious Life Among the White Working Class', *Research in the Sociology of Work* 23 (2012), 227–50; Tobias Preis *et al.*, 'Quantifying the Behavior of Stock Correlations Under Market Stress', *Scientific Reports* 2 (2012); Carles Boix, Michael Miller, and Sebastian Rosato, 'A Complete Data Set of Political Regimes, 1800–2007', *Comparative Political Studies* 46 (2013), 1523–54; Peter H. Lindert and Jeffrey G. Williamson, 'American Incomes Before and After the Revolution', *The Journal of Economic History* 73 (2013), 725–65.

23 Allen *et al.*, 'Preliminary Global Price Comparisons, 1500–1870'; Konstantinos M. Andreadis *et al.*, 'Twentieth-Century Drought in the Conterminous United States', *Journal of Hydrometeorology* 6 (2005), 985–1001; Kees Klein Goldewijk, 'Three Centuries of Global Population Growth: A Spatial Referenced Population (Density) Database for 1700–2000', *Population and Environment* 26 (2005), 343–67; Kyle F. Davis *et al.*, 'Global Spatio-Temporal Patterns in Human Migration: A Complex Network Perspective', *PLoS ONE* 8 (2013): e53723; Manning, 'Historical Datasets on Africa and the African Atlantic', 604–7; Zeev Maoz and Errol A. Henderson, 'The World Religion Dataset, 1945–2010: Logic, Estimates, and Trends', *International Interactions* 39 (2013), 265–91.

24 David Eltis and David Richardson, *Atlas of the Transatlantic Slave Trade* (New Haven, 2010): www.slavevoyages.org/tast/index.faces.

25 Blair, *Too Much to Know*, 2, crediting the invention of the term 'information age' to Fritz Machlup, *The Production and Distribution of Knowledge in the United States* (Princeton, NJ, 1962).

26 Robert William Fogel and Stanley L. Engerman, 'The Relative Efficiency of Slavery: A Comparison of Northern and Southern Agriculture in 1860', *Explorations in Economic History* 8 (1971), 353–67; Fogel and Engerman, *Time on the Cross: The Economics of American Negro Slavery* (Boston, 1974); Fogel, 'The Limits of Quantitative Methods in History', *The American Historical Review* 80 (1975), 329–50; Herbert G. Gutman, *Slavery and the Numbers Game: A Critique of Time on the Cross* (Urbana, 1975); Samuel P. Hays, 'Scientific versus Traditional History: The Limitations of the Current Debate', *Historical Methods: A Journal of Quantitative and Interdisciplinary History* 17 (1984), 75–8; Fogel, *The Slavery Debates, 1952–1990: A Retrospective* (Baton Rouge, LA, 2003).

27 Christopher Dyer, 'Poverty and Its Relief in Late Medieval England', *Past & Present* 216 (2012), 41–78. Other experiments with probate records have tested which religious denomination was preferred by the wealthiest individuals in the nineteenth century.

28 Thomas N. Maloney, 'Migration and Economic Opportunity in the 1910s: New Evidence on African-American Occupational Mobility in the North', *Explorations in Economic History* 38 (2001), 147–65; Maloney, 'Ghettos and Jobs in History: Neighborhood Effects on African American Occupational Status and Mobility in World War I-Era Cincinnati', *Social Science History* 29 (2005), 241–67.

29 J. Foweraker and R. Krznaric, 'How to Construct a Database of Liberal Democratic Performance', *Democratization* 8 (2001), 1–25; Scott Gates *et al.*, 'Institutional Inconsistency and Political Instability: Polity Duration, 1800–2000', *American Journal of Political Science* 50 (2006), 893–908; Lee B. Becker, Tudor Vlad, and Nancy Nusser, 'An Evaluation of Press Freedom Indicators', *International Communication Gazette* 69 (2007), 5–28.

30 Sara McLaughlin *et al.*, 'Timing the Changes in Political Structures: A New Polity Database', *The Journal of Conflict Resolution* 42 (1998), 231–42; Tatu Vanhanen, 'A New Dataset for Measuring Democracy, 1810–1998', *Journal of Peace Research* 37 (2000), 251–65; Nils Petter Gleditsch *et al.*, 'Armed Conflict 1946–2001: A New Dataset', *Journal of Peace Research* 39 (2002), 615–37; Andreas Wimmer and Brian Min, 'The Location and Purpose of Wars Around the World: A New Global Dataset, 1816–2001', *International Interactions* 35 (2009), 390–417; Michael A. Elliott, 'The Institutional Expansion of Human Rights, 1863–2003: A Comprehensive Dataset of International Instruments', *Journal of Peace Research* 48 (2011), 537–46.

31 Jeffrey G. Williamson, *Winners and Losers over Two Centuries of Globalization* (National Bureau of Economic Research, 2002): www.nber.org. revproxy.brown.edu/papers/w9161; Peter H. Lindert and Jeffrey G.

Williamson, 'Does Globalization Make the World More Unequal?', in *Globalization in Historical Perspective* (University of Chicago Press, 2003), 227–76: www.nber.org.revproxy.brown.edu/chapters/c9590.pdf; David R. Green *et al.*, *Men, Women, and Money: Perspectives on Gender, Wealth, and Investment 1850–1930* (Oxford, 2011); Emily R. Merchant, Brian Gratton, and Myron P. Gutmann, 'A Sudden Transition: Household Changes for Middle Aged US Women in the Twentieth Century', *Population Research and Policy Review* 31 (2012), 703–26; Peter H. Lindert and Jeffrey G. Williamson, *American Incomes 1774–1860* (National Bureau of Economic Research, 2012): www.nber.org.revproxy.brown.edu/papers/w18396; John Parman, 'Good Schools Make Good Neighbors: Human Capital Spillovers in Early 20th Century Agriculture', *Explorations in Economic History* 49 (2012), 316–34; 'Intergenerational Occupational Mobility in Great Britain and the United States Since 1850: Comment', *The American Economic Review* 103 (2013), 2021–40; Jan Luiten van Zanden *et al.*, 'The Changing Shape of Global Inequality 1820–2000; Exploring a New Dataset', *Review of Income and Wealth* 60 (2014), 279–97.

32 Massimo A. Bollasina, Yi Ming, and V. Ramaswamy, 'Earlier Onset of the Indian Monsoon in the Late Twentieth Century: The Role of Anthropogenic Aerosols', *Geophysical Research Letters* 40 (2013), 3715–20.

33 Aiguo Dai, Kevin E. Trenberth, and Taotao Qian, 'A Global Dataset of Palmer Drought Severity Index for 1870–2002: Relationship with Soil Moisture and Effects of Surface Warming', *Journal of Hydrometeorology* 5 (2004), 1117–30; Francisco Alvarez-Cuadrado and Markus Poschke, 'Structural Change Out of Agriculture: Labor Push versus Labor Pull', *American Economic Journal: Macroeconomics* 3 (2011), 127–58; Urs Gimmi, Thibault Lachat, and Matthias Bürgi, 'Reconstructing the Collapse of Wetland Networks in the Swiss Lowlands 1850–2000', *Landscape Ecology* 26 (2011), 1071–83; Hans de Moel, Jeroen C. J. H. Aerts, and Eric Koomen, 'Development of Flood Exposure in the Netherlands during the 20th and 21st Century', *Global Environmental Change*, Special Issue on The Politics and Policy of Carbon Capture and Storage, 21 (2011), 620–7; Tello and Badía-Miró, 'Land-Use Profiles of Agrarian Income and Land Ownership Inequality in the Province of Barcelona'; Benjamin S. Felzer, 'Carbon, Nitrogen, and Water Response to Climate and Land Use Changes in Pennsylvania During the 20th and 21st Centuries', *Ecological Modelling* 240 (2012), 49–63; Peter Sandholt Jensen and Tony Vittrup Sørensen, 'Land Inequality and Conflict in Latin America in the Twentieth Century', *Defence and Peace Economics* 23 (2012), 77–94; Robert H. Bates and Steven A. Block, 'Revisiting African Agriculture: Institutional Change and Productivity Growth', *The Journal of Politics* 75 (2013), 372–84.

34 Amartya Sen, *Poverty and Famines: An Essay on Entitlement and Deprivation* (Oxford, 1981).

35 Álvaro Franco, Carlos Álvarez-Dardet, and Maria Teresa Ruiz, 'Effect of Democracy on Health: Ecological Study', *British Medical Journal* 329 (2004), 1421–3.

36 M. Rodwan Abouharb and Anessa L. Kimball, 'A New Dataset on Infant Mortality Rates, 1816–2002', *Journal of Peace Research* 44 (2007), 743–54; Tanya L. Blasbalg *et al.*, 'Changes in Consumption of Omega-3 and Omega-6 Fatty Acids in the United States During the 20th Century', *The American Journal of Clinical Nutrition* 93 (2011), 950–62; Jean M. Twenge, 'Generational Differences in Mental Health: Are Children and Adolescents Suffering More, or Less?', *The American Journal of Orthopsychiatry* 81 (2011), 469–72; Johan P. Mackenbach, Yannan Hu, and Caspar W. N. Looman, 'Democratization and Life Expectancy in Europe, 1960–2008', *Social Science & Medicine* 93 (2013), 166–75.

37 Joerg Baten and Matthias Blum, 'Why Are You Tall While Others Are Short? Agricultural Production and Other Proximate Determinants of Global Heights', *European Review of Economic History* 18 (2014), 144–65.

38 'Declassification Engine': www.declassification-engine.org/.

39 R. Rudy Higgens-Evenson, 'Financing a Second Era of Internal Improvements: Transportation and Tax Reform, 1890–1929', *Social Science History* 26 (2002), 623–51. Higgens-Evenson uses data from Richard Sylla, John B. Legler, and John Wallis, *Sources and Uses of Funds in State and Local Governments, 1790–1915* (machine-readable dataset) (Ann Arbor, MI, 1995), who archived their data at the Interuniversity Consortium for Political and Social Research (ICPSR).

40 http://landmatrix.org/en/about/.

41 http://offshoreleaks.icij.org/search; https://wikileaks.org/; Nicholas Shaxson, *Treasure Islands: Tax Havens and the Men Who Stole the World* (London, 2011).

42 Rosemary Randall, 'Loss and Climate Change: The Cost of Parallel Narratives', *Ecopsychology* 1 (2009), 118–29.

43 Adrian M. Lister, 'Natural History Collections as Sources of Long-Term Datasets', *Trends in Ecology & Evolution* 26 (2011), 153–4; Ryan Tucker Jones, *Empire of Extinction: Russians and the North Pacific's Strange Beasts of the Sea, 1741–1867* (New York, 2014).

44 http://seen.co/.

45 https://www.recordedfuture.com/.

46 Quentin Hardy, 'Crushing the Cost of Predicting the Future', Bits Blog, *The New York Times*: http://bits.blogs.nytimes.com/2011/11/17/crushing-the-cost-of-predicting-the-future/?_php=true&_type=blogs&_r=0.

47 Stephan de Spiegeleire, personal correspondence to Jo Guldi (2 January 2014).

48 Lea Berrang-Ford, James D. Ford, and Jaclyn Paterson, 'Are We Adapting to Climate Change?', *Global Environmental Change* 21 (2011), 25–33.

49 Zachary Karabell, *The Leading Indicators: A Short History of the Numbers That Rule Our World* (New York, 2014), 44.

50 Tatu Vanhanen, 'A New Dataset Compared with Alternative Measurements of Democracy', in Hans-Joachim Lauth, Gert Pickel, and Christian Welzel (eds.), *Demokratiemessung: Konzepte und Befunde im internationalen Vergleich* (Wiesbaden, 2000), 184–206.

51 Karabell, *The Leading Indicators*, 125, 130–5, 147–9.

52 Richard Grove and Vinita Damodaran, 'Imperialism, Intellectual Networks, and Environmental Change: Unearthing the Origins and Evolution of Global Environmental History', in Sverker Sörlin and Paul Warde (eds.), *Nature's End: History and the Environment* (Basingstoke, 2009), 23–49; Sörlin and Warde, 'The Problem of the Problem of Environmental History: A Re-Reading of the Field', *Environmental History* 12 (2007), 107–30.

53 Harold Perkin, *The Third Revolution: Professional Elites in the Modern World* (London, 1996); Max Weber, *Science as a Vocation* (1917), in Weber, *The Vocation Lectures* (ed.) David Owen and Tracy B. Strong (Indianapolis, 2004), 1–31.

54 Frédéric Lebaron, 'Economists and the Economic Order: The Field of Economists and the Field of Power in France', *European Societies* 3 (2001), 91–110; Stephen Turner, 'What Is the Problem with Experts?', *Social Studies of Science* 31 (2001), 123–49.

55 Karl R. Popper, *The Poverty of Historicism* (New York, 1961); Hayden White, *Metahistory: The Historical Imagination in Nineteenth-Century Europe* (Baltimore, 1975).

56 Alberto Alesina, Paola Giuliano, and Nathan Nunn, 'On the Origins of Gender Roles: Women and the Plough', *The Quarterly Journal of Economics* 128 (2013), 469–530.

57 Diego Comin, William Easterly, and Erik Gong, *Was the Wealth of Nations Determined in 1000 BC?* (National Bureau of Economic Research, 2006): www.nber.org/papers/w12657.ack. See also Enrico Spolaore and Romain Wacziarg, *Long-Term Barriers to Economic Development* (National Bureau of Economic Research, 2013): www.nber.org/papers/w19361.

58 Boyd Hilton, *The Age of Atonement: The Influence of Evangelicalism on Social and Economic Thought, 1785–1865* (Oxford, 1992).

59 Marshall Sahlins, *Stone Age Economics* (Chicago, 1972); David Graeber, *Toward an Anthropological Theory of Value: The False Coin of Our Own Dreams* (New York, 2001); Graeber, 'A Practical Utopian's Guide to the Coming Collapse', *The Baffler* 22 (2013), 23–35.

60 Geoffrey M. Hodgson, 'Darwin, Veblen and the Problem of Causality in Economics', *History and Philosophy of the Life Sciences* 23 (2001), 385–423.

61 James Vernon, *Distant Strangers: How Britain Became Modern* (Berkeley, 2014), 133.

62 The most formal postulation of this argument is by William H. Sewell, Jr, *Logics of History: Social Theory and Social Transformation* (Chicago, 2005); George Steinmetz, '"Logics of History" as a Framework for an Integrated Social Science', *Social Science History* 32 (2008), 535–53. For an alternative set of causes particularly appropriate to the Anthropocene, see J. Donald Hughes, 'Three Dimensions of Environmental History', *Environment and History* 14 (2008), 319–30.

63 Compare David J. Staley, *History and Future: Using Historical Thinking to Imagine the Future* (Lanham, MD, 2007) for parallels between the multicausality of the past and the open-endedness of multiple futures.

64 For some recent examples, see Helen Shenton, 'Virtual Reunification, Virtual Preservation and Enhanced Conservation', *Alexandria* 21 (2009), 33–45; David Zeitlyn, 'A Dying Art? Archiving Photographs in Cameroon', *Anthropology Today* 25 (2009), 23–6; Clifford Lynch, 'Defining a National Library in a Digital World: Dame Lynne Brindley at the British Library', *Alexandria* 23 (2012), 57–63; Jian Xu, 'A Digitization Project on Dongjing: Redefining Its Concept and Collection', *Microform and Digitization Review* 41 (2012), 83–6; Tjeerd de Graaf, 'Endangered Languages and Endangered Archives in the Russian Federation', in David Singleton, Joshua A. Fishman, Larissa Aronin, and Muiris Ó Laoire (eds.), *Current Multilingualism: A New Linguistic Dispensation* (Berlin, 2013), 279–96; John Edward Philips, 'The Early Issues of the First Newspaper in Hausa Gaskiya Ta Fi Kwabo, 1939–1945', *History in Africa* 41 (2014), 425–31.

65 Simon Schama, 'If I Ruled the World', *Prospect* (21 August 2013): www.prospectmagazine.co.uk/magazine/if-i-ruled-the-world-september-2013-simon-schama/#.U7SBrKjXqBw.

CONCLUSION: THE PUBLIC FUTURE OF THE PAST

1 Sanford M. Jacoby, 'History and the Business School', *Labour History* 98 (2010), 212.

2 Peter Suber, *Open Access* (Cambridge, MA, 2012); Martin Paul Eve, *Open Access and the Humanities: Contexts, Controversies and the Future* (Cambridge, 2014).

3 Lynn Hunt, *Writing History in the Global Era* (New York, 2014), 120.

4 James C. Scott, *The Art of Not Being Governed: An Anarchist History of Upland Southeast Asia* (New Haven, 2009).

5 Matti Peltonen, 'Clues, Margins, and Monads: The Micro–Macro Link in Historical Research', *History and Theory* 40 (2001), 347–59; Marshall Sahlins, 'Structural Work: How Microhistories Become Macrohistories and Vice Versa', *Anthropological Theory* 5 (2005), 5–30.

6 For an exemplary application of just this method, which pays homage to Braudel and the *longue durée*, see Saliha Belmessous, *Assimilation and Empire: Uniformity in French and British Colonies, 1541–1954* (Oxford, 2013); see also David Armitage, 'What's the Big Idea? Intellectual History and the *Longue Durée*', *History of European Ideas* 38 (2012), 493–507, for the parallel conception of 'serial contextualism' in *longue-durée* intellectual history.

7 Paul Carter, *The Road to Botany Bay: An Essay in Spatial History* (London, 1987), xxiii. Carter takes the image from James Boswell's *Journal*.

8 John Markoff and Verónica Montecinos, 'The Ubiquitous Rise of Economists', *Journal of Public Policy* 13 (1993), 37–68.

9 http://republicofletters.stanford.edu/; Patricia Cohen, 'Humanities Scholars Embrace Digital Technology', *New York Times* (16 November 2010): www.nytimes.com/2010/11/17/arts/17digital.html; Cohen, 'Digitally Mapping the Republic of Letters', *New York Times Artsbeat Blog* (16 November 2010): http://artsbeat.blogs.nytimes.com/2010/11/16/digitally-mapping-the-republic-of-letters.

10 Jerome de Groot, 'Empathy and Enfranchisement: Popular Histories', *Rethinking History* 10 (2006), 391–413.

11 Andrew Davies and Julie-Marie Strange, 'Where Angels Fear to Tread: Academics, Public Engagement and Popular History', *Journal of Victorian Culture* 15 (2010), 268–79.

12 Pamela Cox, 'The Future Uses of History', *History Workshop Journal* 75 (2013), 17–18.

13 Craig Calhoun, 'Social Science for Public Knowledge', in Sven Eliaeson and Ragnvald Kalleberg (eds.), *Academics as Public Intellectuals* (Newcastle upon Tyne, 2008), 299–318.

14 Fernand Braudel, 'Préface' (1946), in *La Méditerranée et le Monde méditerranéen à l'époque de Philippe II* (Paris, 1949), xiv.

15 J. Franklin Jameson, 'The Future Uses of History', *American Historical Review* 65 (1959), 70, quoted in Cox, 'The Future Uses of History', 18.

Index

activism 101–2
Acton, John Emerich Edward Dalberg 49
'Age of Fracture' (Rodgers) 52–3
agriculture
  reductionist theories of 109
  sustainable 32–5
Ahlberg, Christopher 103–4
American Historical Review 47
Amis, Kingsley 49–50
Annales (journal) 15
Annales School 16, 45
Anthropocene 65, 69, 86
anthropology 120
  economic 79
anti-globalisation movements 76–7
apocalyptic thinking 62
archival studies 43–5
  of invisible/forbidden data 100–3
Augustine 19

Bailyn, Bernard 53
Barker, Rodney 52
Barles, Sabine 67–8
Beard, Charles 25
Berger, Gaston 18
Bew, Paul 51–2
biases
  on civilisations 108
  in data analysis 106–8, 110
big data
  analysis of
    biases in 106–8, 110
    critical 111–12, 115
    by historians 107–15
    tools for 89–95, 103–4, 115
  availability of 63, 95–100
    invisible/forbidden 100–3
  preservation of 113

use of 80, 114–16
  in climate change studies 95–6, 99, 105
  in historical studies 55–6, 66–8, 80–1,
    88–9, 93–5
  in political science 74, 98–9, 106
  in social sciences 88
  in university education 104–7
Big History 8–9, 86, 119–20
biographies 48–9
biology, evolutionary 109
Bourdieu, Pierre 9
Brand, Stewart 2
Braudel, Fernand 9–10, 15–19, 124
Brundtland Commission 33

Calhoun, Craig 124
Cambridge School of intellectual history 48
Cannadine, David 53
capitalism
  alternatives for 75
  inequality reduction by 57–60, 79–81, 122–3
carrying capacity 72
  see also sustainability
Carson, Rachel 62
Carter, Paul 121
Chandler, Alfred Noblit 28
change
  awareness of 3–5
  historians on 14, 123
  historical studies used for promotion of
    41–2
church historians 19
Churchill, Winston 14
Cicero 19
cities, history of 43, 67–8
civilisations
  biases on 108
  clash of 74

Clark, Greg 60
'clash of civilisations' thesis (Huntington) 74
classics, history writing in 19
climate change studies 30–1, 61–3
  big data used in 95–6, 99, 105
  economists' views of 63, 66
  and future thinking by historians 61–73
  reductionism in 63–4
cliometrics 97–8
Club of Rome 61–2
Collapse: How Societies Choose to Fail or Succeed (Diamond) 57
commons, tragedy of the 61
communism, end of 73–4
conflicts, cultural 74
Connelly, Matthew 101
contextualism 48
corporate power 78–9
counterfactual thinking 31–4
Cox, Pamela 123
crises
  ecological 143
  of humanities 5–7, 15–16
critical history 14–15, 54, 72, 119–20
Crutzen, Paul 65
cultures
  capitalist 75
  conflicts of 74

Dark Archives 100–3
data *see* big data
Debt: The First 5000 Years (Graeber) 75
debt, historical studies of 75
'Declassification Engine' 101
Deep History 8–9, 86, 120
democracy
  and expert rule 78
  and famine aversion 99–100
  measurements of 106
  and technological development 77–8
destiny, thinking about 30–1
Diamond, Jared 57
digital humanities 88–95
'dirty' *longue durée* 28–9
Dyer, Christopher 98

ecological crises
  in Europe 143
  see also climate change studies
economic anthropology 79

economic governance 76
economic growth
  and climate change 71
  limits of 109–10
economic history 57–60, 75, 78–9, 99
economic well-being, measurement of 106
economics 110, 121–2
economists
  on climate change studies 63, 66
  on inequality and capitalism 57–60, 79–81, 122–3
  Malthusianism of 109–10
  predominance of 11–12
education, university 104–7
  history teaching 38–9, 43, 51, 112
Eley, Geoff 39, 41–3, 45
'end of history' thesis (Fukuyama) 74
Engerman, Stanley 97–8
Epstein, Leon D. 52
Europe, ecological crises in 143
evolutionary biology 109
expert rule 78
extensibility 94–5

Fabian socialism 21–3
famine, aversion of, and democracy 99–100
Fasolt, Constantin 85
Financial Times 80
Fogel, Robert 97–8
forbidden data 100–3
fossil economy, foundations of 70–1
Foucault, Michel 50
free will 30–1
Freedom House 106
Friendly, Michael 94
Fukuyama, Francis 74
future thinking through history 4–5, 12–14, 29–35, 117, 123–5
  and climate change studies 64–73
  and *longue-durée* history 61–3, 117–18
futurology 3–4, 18

George, Henry 27–8
global governance
  and climate change 71
  and *longue-durée* history 73–9
global history 15
globalisation 36, 73–4
Goodman, Paul 42
Google Ngrams 93
governance
  economic 76

global
    and climate change 71
    and *longue-durée* history 73–9
Graeber, David 75
Graves, Robert 49
Great Britain, Victorian period 57–60
Green, William A. 55
Grendi, Edoardo 46
growth, economic
    and climate change 71
    limits of 109–10
Guldi, Jo 90–3

Habermas, Jürgen 50
Hardin, Garrett 61
Heffer, Jean 54
historians
    inequality opposed by 21
    as information designers 114
    job market for 42–5
    as rebels 42
    university education of 38–9, 43, 51, 112
History of Mankind (UNESCO) 82
history/history writing 7, 60
    critical 14–15, 54, 72, 119–20
    deep 8–9, 86, 120
    economic 57–60, 75, 78–9, 99
    and future thinking 4–5, 12–14, 29–35,
        117–18, 123–5
    and climate change studies 61–73
    global 15
    long-termism in *see longue-durée* history
    micro- 11, 98, 113
        and *longue-durée* history 35–6, 46, 50–1,
        120–1
    and macro-history 119–20
    and Short Past 40, 45–7, 83
    military 21
    by non-historians 29
    periods
        classics 19
        middle ages 19
        modernity 19–20
    public responsibility of 117–19, 123, 125
    research
        big data 55–6, 66–8, 80–1, 88–9, 93–5
        data analysis 107–15
        political goals of 20–9, 57–60
        quantitative methods 97–8
        visualisations 122–3
    short-termism in *see* Short Past
    as story-telling 56

and time 15–17
    'turns' in 47
    urban 43, 67–8
Hobsbawm, Eric 24, 41–2
Hodgson, Geoffrey 110
Hornborg, Alf 70–1
Horrell, Sara 59–60
Hulme, Mike 31
humanities
    crises of 5–7, 15–16
    digital 88–95
Hunt, Lynn 6, 119
Huntington, Samuel 74

inequality
    capitalism's reduction of 57–60, 79–81, 99,
        122–3
    historians fighting against 21
    and *longue-durée* history 79–81
information design, by historians 114
information overload 88, 104–5
International Land Coalition 101–2
invisibility of data 100–3

Jackson, Wes 32, 34
Jacoby, Sanford 118–19
Jameson, J. Franklin 125
job market, for historians 42–5

Kahn, Herman 29
Karabell, Zachary 106–7
keyword searching 89–90, 105
King, Russell 27
Korula, Tarikh 103
Kuznets, Simon 79–80

Lamy, Pascal 2–3
Land and the National Question (Bew) 51–2
land ownership, historical studies of 27–8,
        91–3
Land Tenure and Land Taxation in America
    (Sakolski) 28
Land Title Origins: A Tale of Force and Fraud
    (Chandler) 28
Landa, Manuel de 36
Landes, David 27
The Late Great Planet Earth (Carson) 62
League of Nations 76
Limits to Growth (Club of Rome) 61–2
The Long Land War (Guldi) 91–3
Long Now Foundation 2
The Long Week-End (Graves) 49

longue-durée history 8–10, 13, 15–19
    and big data 88, 93–5, 114–15
    and change/turning points 3–4, 36–7
    'dirty' 28–9
    and future thinking 61–73, 117–18
        on climate change 64–73
    and inequality debates 79–81
    and international governance thinking
        73–9
    and micro-history 35–6, 46, 50–1, 120–1
    mythologies destructed by 79, 81–2
    need for 4, 54–7, 125
    political use of 20–9
    retreat of 39–40, 42–3, 48–53, 82–4
    return of 8–10, 13, 34–5, 37, 48, 84–7
Lucky Jim (Amis) 49–50

Machiavelli, Niccolò 20
macro-history
    by anthropologists 120
    and micro-history 119–20
MALLET (software) 91
Malm, Andreas 70–1
Maloney, Thomas 98
Malthusianism 109–10
ManyEyes 93
Mapping of the Republic of Letters Project
    (Stanford University) 122
Markandya, Anil 66
Martin Commission 2–4
McCoy, Florence 51
McNeill, William H. 36
*La Méditerranée et le Monde méditerranéen
    à l'époque de Philippe II* (Braudel) 16
metanarratives 108
micro-history 11, 98, 113
    and *longue durée* 35–6, 46, 50–1, 120–1
    and macro-history 119–20
    and Short Past 40, 45–7, 83
Middle Ages, historical writings in 19
military history 21
modern history 19–20
Moretti, Franco 93
Mumford, Lewis 26, 34
mythologies, destruction of
    by *longue-durée* history 79, 81–2
    by Short Past 55

Naaman, Mor 103
narratives, meta 108
national histories 25
neo-liberalism 73–4

New Roots for Agriculture (Jackson) 34
NGOs, data collection by 101–2
non-historians, historical writings by 29
Novick, Peter 53–4
Now for the Long Term (Lamy et al.) 2–4

Orr, John Boyd 27
Our Common Future (Brundtland
    Commission) 33
Oxford Martin Commission *see* Martin
    Commission

Palmer, R. R. 53
Paper Machines (software) 90–3, 104
Paris, history of 67–8
Perkin, Harold 108
Persson, Karl 60
Piketty, Thomas 79–81, 122–3
political goals/policy-making, historical
    studies used for 20–9, 57–60
political science, big data used in 74, 98–9,
    106
Polity Project 106
population control 72–3
preservation, of data 113
public responsibility
    of historical studies 117–19, 123, 125
    of social sciences 123–4

quantitative methods, use in historical
    research 97–8

racism 55, 98
rebellion 42
Recorded Future 103–4
reductionism
    in economics 57–60
    in evolutionary biology 109
    time-related 63–4
research
    digitally driven 89–95
    historical
        data analysis in 107–15
        political goals of 20–9, 57–60
        quantitative methods 97–8
    visualisations of 121–3
responsibility
    public
        of historical studies 117–19, 123, 125
        of social sciences 123–4
    of West for climate change 71, 73
Robin, Libby 65, 69

Rodgers, Daniel 52–3
Roman empire, historical writings in 19

Saez, Emmanuel 81
Sakolski, Aaron 28
Sayre, Nathan 72
Schama, Simon 116
Schlesinger, Arthur, Jr 26–7
Schlesinger, Arthur, Sr 25, 52
Schmidt, Ben 93
Scott, James C. 120
Seen.Co (website) 103
Sen, Amartya 99–100
Short Past 7–8, 11, 17, 39–40, 42–53
    contribution of 55, 57
    criticism of 51–4
    dominance of 82
    and micro-history 40, 45–7, 83
    and social change 41–2
    in university education 51
short-termism 1–3, 81–2
Skinner, Quentin 47–8
Smail, Daniel Lord 84
social sciences 17, 83
    big data in 88
    public responsibility of 123–4
    see also anthropology; political science
socialism
    demise of 73–4
    Fabian 21–3
software, for text mining 90–3, 104
space, and history 15
specialisation, criticism of 49–50
Spence, Michael 5
states, Westphalian system of 76
steam technology 70–1
The Story of Utopias (Mumford) 34
story-telling, history as 56
students of history *see* historians, university
    education of
sustainability 32–4, 69
    and *longue-durée* history 34–5, 68–9

Tawney, R. H. 23–4
technological development
    and participatory democracy 77–8
    steam technology 70–1
temporalities *see* time
text mining tools 90–3, 104
Thirsk, Joan 68

Thompson, Paul B. 33, 68
Thucydides 19
time
    and data analysis 107
    and history 15–17
    reductionism in analyses of 63–4
    'Tragedy of the commons' (article, Hardin)
        61
Tuma, Elias 27
turning-points, in *longue-durée* history
        36–7
'turns', historical 47
Tvedt, Terje 67

unemployment statistics, short-term biases in
        106
UNESCO, *History of Mankind* project
        82
United Nations 76
United States
    academic history teaching in 43
    historical writings in 25–7, 78–9
universities
    crises of 5–7
    longevity of 5–6
    teaching at
        big data used in 104–7
        of history 38–9, 43, 51, 112
    urban history 43, 67–8
    utopian thinking 34–5

Vernon, James 86, 110
visualisations of research results 121–2
    of historical studies 122–3

Warde, Paul 66–7
Ware, Caroline 82
water, history of 67
Webb, Beatrice and Sidney 21–3
Weber, Max 108
West
    perceived superiority of 55, 70–1
    responsibility for climate change 71, 73
Westphalian state system 76
white superiority myth 55
Williams, William Appleman 27
Windelband, Wilhelm 14–15
World Bank 76

Yates, Joshua J. 69

Printed in the United States
by Baker & Taylor Publisher Services